# THE ULTIMATE MARKETING PLAN

*Find Your Hook.*
*Communicate Your Message.*
*Make Your Mark.*

Dan S. Kennedy

## third edition

**BUSINESS**
**Adams Business**
Avon, Massachusetts

"I finally got a minute to write a letter to convey my heartfelt appreciation for everything you've done to change my life. It's your own fault that I haven't had time to write. That's because I'm so busy trying to drink from the fire hose of leads and business you've created for me. While most other mortgage brokers are starving in this current environment, I'm having my best month ever—fees and commissions over $77,000.00, and $67,000.00 is NET thanks to the unusual way I do business. It's important to point out I have zero employees and work less than 40 hours a week!"

**Scott Tucker**
Mortgage Business, Illinois

......

"Here are the results of our new ads and mailing pieces following your advice: price shoppers have disappeared. We close almost everyone who calls now. In fact, we ask them two questions to see if they qualify to be our customer!"

**Ron & Tina Guidetti**
Absolute Best Carpet Cleaning, Massachusetts

......

"Results from one year to the next: increased sales by 21%, 1,221 new customers, a $7,000.00 savings in advertising costs, increased each customer's value, and increased new customers' return visits within the first 30 days."

**Dennis Babjack**
Washington Street Mercantile, Ohio

......

"A 340% increase in sales over 4 years, from $735,000.00 to $2,500,000.00. Thank you Dan Kennedy!"

**Don Gordon**
SWL Crane & Hoist Ltd., Ontario, Canada

......

"No one knows more ways to get customers than Dan Kennedy."

**Rory Fatt**
Restaurant Marketing Systems, Vancouver, B.C.

Published by Adams Media, an F+W Publications Company
57 Littlefield Street
Avon, MA 02322
*www.adamsmedia.com*

Printed in the United States of America.

J I H G F E D

ISBN 10: 1-59337-496-8
ISBN 13: 978-1-59337-496-9
Kennedy, Dan S.
The ultimate marketing plan : find your hook. communicate your message.
make your mark. / Dan S. Kennedy.—3rd ed.
p. cm.
ISBN 1-59337-496-8
1. Marketing—United States. 2. Sales promotion—United States.
3. Direct marketing—United States. I. Title.
HF5415.1.K37 2006
658.8'02—dc22
2005026071

The Publisher of this work is in no way responsible for the National Sales Letter Contest or any other contest affiliated with this book or the author. All contest rules, fulfillment, liability, and indemnity are the sole responsibility of the author of this work, Dan S. Kennedy.

This publication is designed to provide accurate and authoritative information with regard to the subject matter covered. It is sold with the understanding that the publisher is not engaged in rendering legal, accounting, or other professional advice. If legal advice or other expert assistance is required, the services of a competent professional person should be sought.
—From a *Declaration of Principles* jointly adopted by a Committee of the American Bar Association and a Committee of Publishers and Associations

Many of the designations used by manufacturers and sellers to distinguish their product are claimed as trademarks. Where those designations appear in this book and Adams Media was aware of a trademark claim, the designations have been printed with initial capital letters.

Interior design and composition by
Electronic Publishing Services, Inc. (Tennessee)

This book is available at quantity discounts for bulk purchases.
For information, please call 1-800-289-0963.

# CONTENTS

# How to Get Maximum Value from This Book

## (1)

Throughout the book, you will find little boxes headlined Resource! Many of these direct you to Web sites where you can find examples and demonstrations of strategies presented in the book, or expanded information. For example, on pages 170–171, we discuss the use of robot-delivered voice broadcast messages. In that Resource! box, you'll find a Web site you can go to to hear several actual, successful voice broadcast messages.

## (2)

Let us motivate you to take action! Enter the Ultimate Marketing Plan/ Ultimate Sales Letter Contest and compete for a brand new Ford Mustang and other awards! Go to *www.NationalSalesLetterContest.com*. Entry is free. Contest extends eighteen months from the first publication of this book. After that, there will be a modified, "consolation" competition that will award a prize every six months. However, if you've obtained this book within the initial, main contest term, you'll be able to compete for a Ford Mustang! Go to the site and enter immediately, even before you've read this book, so you get all the information as early as possible and have as much opportunity as possible to participate.

This contest is designed to encourage you to implement the ideas in this book, and its companion book *The Ultimate Sales Letter*; however, purchase of book(s) is NOT required to participate, nor is any other purchase. Contest rules provided at site.

## (3)—FREE BONUS GIFT!

Prepare your own personal ULTIMATE MARKETING PLAN! A complete set of fill-in-the-blank "Think Pages" and an Action Guide are included with the free 12-Week Ultimate Marketing Plan Course delivered by e-mail, at *www.UltimateMarketingPlan.com*.

## (4)—FREE BONUS GIFT!

Keep developing supereffective marketing strategies beyond those presented in the book, and see current examples of these strategies in action, from diverse businesses from all across the country, and even around the world! Register for a free three-month subscription to the author's *No B.S. Marketing Letter* at *www.UltimateMarketingPlan.com*.

# Preface

On airplanes and at cocktail parties, I'm always unsure of what to say when I'm asked what I do. I spend some of my time as a "professional speaker," running around the country getting paid to talk—often about the subject of this book, *The Ultimate Marketing Plan,* and its predecessor and companion book, *The Ultimate Sales Letter.* But I've pretty much given up identifying myself as a "speaker." A lot of people think that's a stereo component, and they start asking me questions about CDs and such.

Often I say I'm a marketing consultant, which I am more than anything else. At a party, one lady who overheard that rushed over. "Really? A marketing consultant? Good. For years I've been wondering and have never had anybody to ask—why does every damned shopping cart have one bad wheel?"

**Well, what is "marketing," anyway?**

**My basic definition is that it is getting the right message to the right people via the right media and methods.**

The purpose of this book is to equip you with the same process that I use as a consultant in helping clients craft the right message for their products, services, or businesses, choose the best media and methods to deliver it, and choose the best prospects to deliver it to.

After you've gone through the book, you can get a fill-in-the-blank Ultimate Marketing Plan Action Guide for your own use, free, online at *www.UltimateMarketingPlan.com.* Personally, I detest planning. I've got the classic entrepreneurial nature—"Ready? FIRE! Aim." So if you start wondering about this book . . . if you start muttering, "Plan? Geez. Let's just go sell something," well, I understand. However, here's my promise to you: if you will honestly take the time to go through this book from start to finish without skimming or skipping, think about what you read, and then get the fill-in-the-blank Plan pages, sit down in a quiet place, and fill them in, you will be more effective, efficient, and successful in whatever business you're in.

Each day, from the minute your prospect awakes until the minute his exhausted eyes close at night, he is bombarded with advertising and marketing messages. On television, on the radio, on the Internet at any Web site he visits, in his e-mail, in his fax machine, on billboards, through his cell phone, in his mailbox at work and at home, and on and on and on. If you accurately count every single time you are marketed to during just one day, you'll find it's in the thousands. This is the clutter and chaos and cacophony you must penetrate just to get your customer's or client's or prospect's attention!

If you successfully get through, you and the others who made it this far then have to compete for the attention, interest, precious time, and dollars of your clientele.

**Dan S. Kennedy**

P.S.: Throughout this book, you'll find "Resources" highlighted. One of the great services I provide my Inner Circle Members and clients is that of clearinghouse and critical filter, to save them time and frustration, directing them to the best people, companies, and sources of reliable information. You will also find a Resource Directory at the end of this book, for your convenience. You can look up individuals, companies, or references mentioned throughout the book by page number in this Directory.

## Other Notes and Acknowledgments

Many of my clients, Glazer-Kennedy Inner Circle Members, and top marketing experts generously provided information and exhibits for this book; notable among them is the publisher of my *No B.S. Marketing*

*Letter,* Bill Glazer. You will see quite a few references to Bill here, as well as exhibits from him. He is an exceptionally astute and successful marketer in several businesses: he owns retail menswear stores, he provides advertising and marketing "tool kits" and coaching to thousands of retailers, he publishes my newsletter, and he has a multimillion-dollar-a-year online catalog business. You will also find a number of contributions here from Mitch Carson, author of *The G.E.N.I.U.S. Direct-Mail Marketing System,* and CEO of Impact Products. Mitch is a speaker and consultant, expert in unique, unusual direct mail using objects, "grabbers," ad specialties, promotional merchandise, premiums, and special packaging. This book also includes contributions from Craig Dickhout, CEO of Think Ink, the leader in personalized direct mail. Corey Rudl, CEO, The Internet Marketing Center, has contributed a bonus chapter. I am indebted to these outstanding experts and to my clients and members, who so freely share their discoveries and successful strategies.

Throughout the book, you will see references to Glazer-Kennedy Inner Circle Members, Gold and Gold+ Glazer-Kennedy Inner Circle Members, and Gold/VIP and Platinum Inner Circle Members. These refer to different levels of members who receive our monthly *No B.S. Marketing Letter,* audio CDs, and other resources, or participate in my elite mastermind/peer advisory coaching groups. Further explanation is at *www.UltimateMarketingPlan.com.*

# Putting Together the Right Message

In 1978, when I started my career as a professional speaker and seminar leader, one of the venerable deans of public speaking, Cavett Robert, sagely cautioned: "Don't be in too much of a hurry to promote, until you get good. Otherwise you just speed up the rate at which the world finds out you're no good." Harsh but good advice. It's been my observation since then that large numbers of businesspeople in all fields rush to promote without stopping long enough to be sure they have something really worth promoting.

A different expression of this same idea is contained in this anonymous poem for advertisers:

> A lion met a tiger
> As they drank beside a pool
> Said the tiger, "Tell me why
> You're roaring like a fool."
>
> "That's not foolish," said the lion
> With a twinkle in his eyes
> "They call me king of all the beasts
> Because I advertise!"
>
> A rabbit heard them talking
> And ran home like a streak
> He thought he'd try the lion's plan,
> But his roar was just a squeak.
>
> A fox came to investigate—
> Had luncheon in the woods.
> Moral: when you advertise, my friends,
> Be sure you've got the goods!

Marketing—and *The Ultimate Marketing Plan*—begins not with any particular media or strategy; it starts with putting together the best, most promotable message possible that truthfully represents "the goods" you've got.

I'm going to suggest a little exercise to you. Stop reading here long enough to get your Yellow Pages telephone directory out and open it up to the business category in which your present or planned business best fits. Start with the first ad and a thick pad of paper. Write down each promise, feature, benefit, and statement in the first advertiser's ad. When you find one of these same statements in the next advertiser's ad, just put a mark next to it, and keep stick-counting the number of times the same statement appears in all of the ads in the section. If you find a new or different statement in any of the ads, add it to your list, then stick-count the number of times it recurs in other ads.

This exercise is instructive for two reasons. First, the Yellow Pages is the most competitive, toughest advertising arena there is. Today, the Internet offers comparable clutter, but there are ways to "pick off" searchers and direct them to looking only at your site. Only in the Yellow Pages is your ad surrounded by your competitors' ads. Your billboard stands alone. Your sales letter or brochure, in the recipient's hands, has exclusive, if momentary, attention. But in the Yellow Pages, your ad is next to, above, below, and/or grouped with all of your competitors' ads. All of you are presenting your messages simultaneously to the same prospective customer. Here, only the strong survive; only the strongest prosper.

Second, in spite of this obvious, extreme competitiveness, your stick-counted list will glaringly reveal one astounding fact: Everybody is saying the same thing. Everybody is delivering the same message.

While this seems to be the way to do things, because that's the way everybody is doing things, it is definitely the wrong approach if you seek exceptional success, even dominance, in your marketplace.

Contrary to all this me-tooism, the "key to the vault" in marketing in general and in this tough medium in particular is a message that differentiates you from all of your competitors in a positive, appealing, preferably compelling way. Many marketing pros call this a "Unique Selling Proposition."

## ULTIMATE MARKETING SECRET WEAPON #1
### The Great USP

A Unique Selling Proposition (USP) is a way of explaining your position against your competition. When a supermarket chain or big-box retailer like Wal-Mart labels itself as "THE Low Price Leader," it's made a positioning promise.

A USP is also a way of summarizing and telegraphing one of the chief benefits, often *the* chief benefit of the business, product, or service being marketed. When I wrote the first edition of this book in the early 1990s, Chrysler was making much out of being the only American carmaker to include driver's-side air bags as standard equipment. That briefly worked for them as a USP, but competition quickly caught up. As I am finishing this new edition, the Subway chain has enjoyed great success repositioning itself as a weight-loss business, first with the story of Jared, one of its customers, and currently by comparing the number of fat grams in its sandwiches to those from McDonald's. How long the company can sustain this is open to question.

Your USP may express the "theme" of your business, product, or service. Think: Which coffee is "mountain grown"? Which beer is made with "the cold, clear water of the Rockies"?

These examples show that a USP can be based on just about anything: price, product ingredient, positioning. There are USPs based on color, size, scent, celebrity endorsement, location, hours of operation, and on and on.

As you concentrate on developing a new USP for your enterprise, you'll be newly aware of the USPs of other businesses, and you can learn from their examples. To hone your marketing mind, you need to become USP-sensitive and ask these questions about every business, product, and service you encounter in your daily activities:

1. Does this business have a USP?
2. If not, can I think of one for it?
3. If so, is there a way I can think of to improve it?
4. Is there any idea here I can "steal" for my use?

# How a Terrific USP Built an Entrepreneurial Empire

I've used this example for more than ten years—it's that good. Once upon a time, two young men determined they would put themselves through college by running a small business. Early on, the business was woefully unsuccessful, and one guy bailed out on the other. The one who stayed and stuck it out came up with a USP that revolutionized his entire industry and made him a multimillionaire. First, his little business grabbed dominant control of the local market; then, rapidly, the state, America, the world!

His USP was: "Fresh, hot pizza delivered in 30 minutes or less, guaranteed." Ten words that brilliantly incorporate two product benefits with the meaningful specific of delivery within thirty minutes—not quick, fast, or soon, but precisely in thirty minutes—and a guarantee. This USP has passed into advertising history, but it fueled the growth of an empire, and thoroughly frustrated competitors large and small. In fact, in its heyday, I played word association with people and asked them to say whatever first popped into their minds when I said "pizza"; 85 out of 100 said "Domino's."

Question: If we went out into your marketplace and asked 100 or 1,000 people to play the game, gave them the generic name for your type of business, and 85 percent of them responded by naming you, how well would you be doing?

I had the privilege of interviewing Tom Monaghan for a magazine article some years ago, and there's no doubt that his success and that of his company have been linked to a complex list of factors, notably including his personal success philosophy and his ability to instill it in his franchisees. But there's also no doubt that his USP was largely responsible for the rapid rise and dominance of his company in the pizza industry. It generated enough wealth to let Tom indulge his lifelong fantasy of buying the Detroit Tigers (with a $53-million-dollar price tag), collect classic cars, give most generously to his church and favorite charities, and be financially independent and secure at a relatively young age.

That is the power of a truly great USP. It *is* worth working on the invention of a strong USP for your product, service, or business. And it's not necessarily easy. I know clients who've taken months, even years, to finally hit on a USP that they liked and that really worked. For each, the months of frustrating brain strain have paid off handsomely.

A good source of ideas is the public library. There, free of charge, you can wander through Yellow Pages directories and newspapers from cities all across the country, as well as hundreds of consumer, business, trade, and specialty magazines. Another source of ideas is the Internet: As you roam cyberspace, visit Web sites within and outside of your business category in search of inspiring USP ideas. Then you can boldly go where few others go, into the marketplace with a really exciting USP of your own!

## Products That Have USP Power

The Christmas shopping season always brings forth a crop of interesting new kitchen appliances; one recent year, it was the Iced Tea Pot. When I first saw this advertised, I burst out laughing. Its manufacturer, the Mr. Coffee Company, went laughing all the way to the bank. Imagine: we can no longer make iced tea in any old kettle; we must have the precisely correct Iced Tea Pot.

It reminds me of a funny phenomenon we have here in the Southwest: the Sun Tea Jar. Because we have searing sunshine every day, it's easy to sun-brew tea just by putting a large jar of water outside for a few hours with tea bags in it. Obviously, any old glass jar will do the job. But on store shelves you'll find large glass jars with the words "Sun Tea Jar" silk-screened on them for sale at four or five times what unmarked jars in the next aisle sell for. And you'll find people cheerfully buying them. After all, what kind of goofball would brew sun tea in a pickle jar?

Some years back, I was president of a fairly large manufacturing company with its own in-house print shop. One day I noticed how much paper was going to waste in the shop, and I brilliantly decreed that the waste be kept and made into pads for the office staff to jot phone messages on, thus eliminating the need to buy those square pads of pink paper imprinted "Phone Message" from the office-supply store. Why, I reasoned, should we buy little pads of paper at retail when we're already buying large truckloads of paper at wholesale?

I almost had a mutiny on my hands. Pointing to the odd-colored, odd-sized pads we got free from our own print shop, the secretaries said, "Those are scratch pads." Holding up the pink imprinted pads from the office-supply store, they said, "These are phone-message pads." End of discussion.

Purely through customized or proprietary appearance, these products have taken on USP POWER that is almost invincible.

If you really want to see this at work, visit an athletic-shoe store. I'm not much of a casual dresser, but, immediately before a day of walking at Disney World, I decided it would be smart to get some comfortable "sneaks." Forty minutes and 85 bucks later, I left the store with a thorough education: there are shoes for walking on pavement, for walking on grass, for walking a lot, for walking a little, for jogging, for tennis, basketball, soccer, football, baseball, trampolining, with pumps, without pumps—but there are no more "sneaks."

Consider these products with USP POWER:

- Microwavable dinners for kids to make for themselves
- Clarion Cosmetics' "computer," which tells you which colors are right for you
- Luzianne iced-tea bags
- A stress management seminar for career women
- A shampoo and conditioner for "swimmer's hair"

_____ **Resource!** _____

For a much longer list of USP ideas, and actual examples from many of my Inner Circle Members and clients, sign up for the free 12-Week Ultimate Marketing Plan e-mail course at *www.UltimateMarketing-Plan.com*. USP is covered in Lesson #2.

And watch the TV commercials for the appetite suppressant products: there's one for people with the urge to binge late in the day, another for people who need help all day, and yet another "extra strength" one—presumably for people with not even a smidgen of willpower.

It's even possible for a mundane product to get USP POWER purely from its package. In 1991, when I wrote the first edition of this book, McDonald's did just that for the cheeseburger with its McDLTs and their hot-side-stays-hot, cold-side-stays-cold, two-bin Styrofoam containers. I think Yuban was the first to provide premeasured filter packs for automatic coffeemakers so you don't have to count out scoops. More recently, cereal companies have put premeasured, single servings of cereal and milk in side-by-side "pockets" of a plastic container stored in the refrigerator.

## To the Prospective Customer's Question, Your USP Is the Answer

When you set out to attract a new, prospective customer to your business for the first time, there is one, paramount question you must answer:

*"Why should I choose your business/product/service versus any/ every other competitive option available to me?"*

I invented this question to help businesspeople "get" USP, and to use as a crowbar to pry ideas out of their heads, to dig out the makings of a good USP. If you can't answer the question, you won't get a USP, but you also have bigger problems; typically, it means that you've been getting your customers only because of the cheapest price, a convenient location, your personal charisma, or the good fortune of being the only provider, and all of these leave you very, very vulnerable to new competition. You need a USP.

I choose to buy Domino's pizza because it's gonna get to me hot, and quickly. I chose the McDLT because my lettuce and tomato stayed cool and crisp. (As you can guess, I miss the McDLT.) I chose Yuban so I didn't have to count scoops. I choose Minit-Lube because I hate hanging around greasy, dirty gas-station waiting areas. Why do I choose the chiropractor I go to? The restaurants I regularly patronize? The dealership where I buy my cars? More often than not, it's because each has USP POWER that appeals to me.

## Boosting USP Power with an Irresistible Offer

I grew up in Ohio and briefly owned an ad agency in a rural community halfway between Cleveland and Akron. At least a dozen times each winter there was enough snow and ice on the country roads to make it ill-advised if not downright impossible to go anywhere. Those days the office stayed closed and I stayed stuck at home.

On one such day, in the midst of a severe blizzard, I stared out my apartment window and watched a neighbor slog through the snow, struggle through the wind, scrape ice from his car's windshield, unfreeze the car's door latch with a cigarette lighter, fight to start the car, and finally slip and slide off into the storm. "I wonder," I asked myself, "what would motivate a guy to go out in weather like this?"

Then I remembered a very similar storm just a couple of winters before when I had quite literally risked my life and badly banged up my car driving all the way from Akron, Ohio, to Murray State University in Kentucky to spend a weekend with my girlfriend of that time. For hours, it snowed so hard I honestly couldn't see past the hood ornament of my car. Every bridge was so icy I spun my way across it. Yet I pressed on.

Waiting for me in Murray, Kentucky, was "an irresistible offer!"

If you can come up with an offer that's irresistible, you are really on to something! Try this one on for size: for $198.00 per person, $396.00 per couple, I'll put you up in a luxurious minisuite in an exciting Las Vegas Hotel, right on the famous strip . . . give you tickets to a show with name entertainers . . . put a chilled bottle of champagne in your room . . . let you drink as much of whatever you want whether you're at the gaming tables, playing the slots, or in one of the lounges . . . give you $1,000.00 of my money to gamble with . . . let you keep all your winnings . . . and as a bonus, guarantee you'll at least win either a color TV, a VCR, or a faux-diamond ring. Obviously I'm not going to give this incredible deal to everybody in the whole world. There can only be a small number of these vacation packages available, first come, first served, and the race is on. Assuming you trust the offer, how fast can you get to a phone and call in to reserve yours? Would you go out in a blizzard and drive to the post office to get your order form in the mail before the deadline?

Well, this was a real offer, from Bob Stupak, the entrepreneurial owner of the original Vegas World Hotel and one of the savviest market-ers I know of to take on Las Vegas. For years, Bob kept his hotel filled to capacity, kept a waiting list going, and got paid months, even years in advance by his guests—all thanks to his invention of this irresistible offer. He used the cash flow generated by selling that "package" to grow his hotel from a tiny, slots-only joint to a huge, two-towered showplace. A few years ago, he sold his interest to a bigger corporation, and Vegas World became the Stratosphere. The Stupak-style marketing ended, and financial troubles multiplied like rabbits in spring.

The Embassy Suites hotel chain has flourished for years and sparked much competition thanks to its offer of "every room a suite," free evening cocktails, and free breakfast.

One of the mail-order catalog companies I occasionally buy from recently sent me a "preferred customer catalog" from which I could buy anything I wanted with "no payments for six months." I confess—I went through that darned catalog looking for something to buy!

One of the classic, often-used irresistible offers is the book and record clubs' "Choose 6 for 10 cents," like the offer shown in Exhibit #1 (page 12).

This exact same offer dates back to records, then eight-track tapes, then cassettes, and now includes CDs. It has stood the test of time for decades! In the marketing of my own *No B.S. Marketing Letter*, I used a knockoff of this "bribe offer" for about ten years, inviting new subscribers to choose any six Special Reports as the free bonus with their subscription. You should make a mental note of this—bonus gifts often drive sales. Now, we've beaten that offer with an even more powerful, outright free trial. The old offer is shown as Exhibit #2 (page 13). You can see the current offer at *www.UltimateMarketingPlan.com*.

## Membership as a USP

What I call "membership concept marketing" has been a very important part of my own business, and it can be a pathway to a USP.

Gold/VIP Member Kevin Fayle, a top marketing consultant to the kitchen remodeling industry, teaches the remodelers in his coaching program to use "membership concept." The remodeler/dealer sells for a fee a Preferred Client Membership, which entitles the members to free design service, free delivery, on-site consultations, decorating advice—and a money-back guarantee on the membership. This is important, because it is impractical to advertise and offer money-back guarantees on customized kitchen installations costing upward from $15,000.00, which cannot readily be resold. With the membership, the dealer gets to use "money-back guarantee" as part of his marketing arsenal.

Kevin says, "Don't dismiss 'membership concept' or guarantees, just because you can't easily see how they apply to your business." And that is very good advice.

## Exhibit #1

## Exhibit #2

<u>**From Dan Kennedy**</u>:
I want to give you the tapes of my latest
Marketing & Moneymaking SuperConference,
which people paid $2,487.00 each to attend,
free.

# FREE:

## 6 Audio Tapes, 5 Special Reports, 1 Book, 2 Critique Certificates, Telephone Consulting & Coaching, a veritable truckload of moneymaking information and assistance.......ALL FREE........ and all you have to do to get all of it is say "maybe."

*Have I finally lost my mind?*

Dear Friend,

Although you have purchased my books or tapes or attended one of my seminars in the past, and although we have previously invited you to subscribe to my NO B.S. MARKETING LETTER, it has been brought to my attention that you are NOT getting my monthly Letter (full to the brim with advice that directly boosts your income, fast) --- and I can<u>not</u> allow that situation to continue, so.....

I am going to bury you in "bribes", just to get you to test-drive my Marketing Letter.

Listen to this: <u>all you have to do is say "*maybe* "</u>............try 3 Issues of my Letter. If that doesn't hook you for life; if you can't see the profit from continuing, you can change your "maybe" to an emphatic "no", and get a full refund plus ten bucks for your trouble. (Details later in this letter.)

Now, let's take a look at the pick-up truck load of "stuff" I have piled up, ready to rush to your doorstep - FREE! - "stuff" that will stimulate your marketing-mind, grease your greed glands, electrify your enthusiasm, <u>point you to overlooked opportunities</u> in your business, <u>hand you ready-to-use and incredibly powerful strategies</u> for magnetically attracting lots of new customers or clients..........selling more, more often to current customers.........one way or another, <u>creating a FLOOD OF MONEY</u> rushing toward YOUR door.

## Being in the Right Place at the Right Time with the Right USP

Once, over a lengthy lunch, I listened to a client, Ned Allen, president of Florida Communities and Intercoastal Communities, two retirement-community firms, reminisce about his starting the famous Steak and Ale restaurants smack in the middle of a national recession. He had started the first restaurant with just $2,000.00, made it successful, and committed to the construction and opening of seven new restaurants just as the recession hit.

Ned said: "We had to quickly change our thinking to match the timing we had to work with. We developed new, lower-cost, higher-perceived-value menu items, and by offering the look, feel, atmosphere, and taste of a gourmet steakhouse at a surprisingly low price, we had the right product at just the right time."

At that time, Ned was not alone in predicting another three- to four-year recession, and he was again busy creating just the right product for it. In this case, the product was a new type of manufactured home for his companies' communities—this one with several hundred square feet less than any other home and, therefore, a substantially lower cost, but with an interior design that made it seem much, much bigger than it was. The home also had lots of nifty "gingerbread" touches that added to its perceived value.

Ned turned his $2,000.00 investment in Steak and Ale into millions when he sold out to Green Giant Foods. He's since made another fortune with his new "Land Yacht" mini retirement home and his inventive approach to low-cost retirement living in Florida.

Of course, it's no secret that timing is a business success factor. But matching a USP with the right timing can dramatically multiply success.

# How "Marketing by Values" Strengthens Your Message

One of my first mentors in business often said: "If you stand for nothing, you'll fall for anything." Just about anything—a recession, new competition—can topple a business devoid of values.

Although there are many great success stories in the fast-food industry, none stand above McDonald's. The McDonald's empire was built on Ray Kroc's unwavering, some would say fanatical, commitment to *consistency*—the idea that the food items at a McDonald's in Iowa are identical to those found under the arches in California. Try to find anything close to this kind of consistency in any other national restaurant chain.

In my opinion, the Holiday Inn chain has lost all touch with its founders' values, but back when I started hitting the road as a frequent business traveler I preferred Holiday Inns for that same reason—consistency. Kemmons Wilson was determined that travelers could depend—*depend*—on Holiday Inns for the basics: clean rooms, safety, courteous service.

Here's another example of a company succeeding through a commitment to values: Federal Express invented, built, and dominated an industry because of a commitment to on-time, as-promised delivery. There are many classic stories of FedEx employees going to extraordinary extremes to keep faith with this fundamental value.

I would suggest, incidentally, that a clearly defined quality appropriate to your business be one of your values. *In Search of Excellence* author Tom Peters jokes about the retail executive who became aggravated at Peters's criticism of his business in a seminar and cried out: "We are no worse than anybody else!" Tom Peters had a graphic artist design a company logo with that slogan in it: We are no worse than anybody else. Unfortunately, many business leaders settle for just this approach.

A client and friend of mind, Don Dwyer, now passed away, built a huge international franchisor organization, encompassing more than 2,000 franchisees in three service industries, from scratch, in just a handful of years—thanks, in a large degree, to his early development of, adherence to, and enthusiastic teaching of a very strong code of values. It goes like this:

1. We believe in superior service to our customers, to our community, and to each other as members of the business community.
2. We believe that if we count our blessings every day, we will keep the negatives away.
3. We believe success is the result of clear, cooperative positive thinking.
4. We believe that in order to build our business we must re-earn our positions every day by excelling in every way.
5. We believe that management should seek out what employees are doing right and treat every associate in a friendly, fair, frank, and firm way.
6. We believe that problems should be welcomed tranquilly and should be used as learning experiences.
7. We believe our Creator put us on this Earth to win. We will keep faith with His wishes by winning honestly and accepting our daily successes humbly, knowing that a higher power has guided us to victory.
8. We believe in the untapped potential of every human being. Every person we help achieve that potential will bring us one step closer to achieving our potential.
9. We believe that loyalty adds consistency to our lives.
10. We believe in building our country through the free-enterprise system. We will demonstrate this belief by constantly attracting people to seek opportunity.

Don did *not* come up with that code *after* making millions, to have an impressive plaque for his office wall. He developed the code in the very infancy of his business, when he was operating out of a small garage (with one truck), telling the few people who would listen that he was going to quickly build a $100-million-a-year corporation. (In short order, he topped $50 million. I'm sure his companies have gone on to get closer and closer to his remarkable, original goal.)

## One Way to Create a Creative USP: Address What Customers *Don't* Like

Steve Fox Plumbing, in California, has this very blunt and straightforward headline in many of its advertisements:

---

**ATTENTION HOMEOWNERS:**
**No other plumber makes you this bold guarantee:**

**"My Plumber Will Smell Good**
**And Show Up On Time**
**Or <u>I Will Pay You</u>."**

---

The company also provides this "Customer Bill Of Rights":

1. You shouldn't have to wait at home all day for a plumber. You deserve our commitment to an appointment time frame.
2. You should expect our plumbers to leave your home as clean and neat after they've finished with your work as when they arrived.
3. You deserve a plumber who is knowledgeable, efficient, pleasant, clean, neat, and of the highest moral character, in your home.
4. You deserve full satisfaction with our products and services or I will redo the repair, free.

Many of my clients and Glazer-Kennedy Inner Circle Members have done fabulous jobs with similar advertising. One of the best is Gold/VIP

Member Bob Higgins of Higgins Painting; you can see full copies of his successful direct-mail pieces and freestanding newspaper inserts when you enroll in the free 12-Week Ultimate Marketing Plan Course, delivered by e-mail, at *www.UltimateMarketingPlan.com*.

## What's Your Magnificent Mission?

The nature and details of my business interests have changed quite a bit over time, but I've always kept them linked to this mission: to be responsible for getting how-to-succeed education into the hands of more people than does any other individual or enterprise.

At one time I saw the implementation of that mission limited to the mail-order marketing of books, cassettes, and courses. Then it expanded to include speaking and seminars. Then television. Then developing products for other publishers. Then consulting with publishers, direct marketers, and even multilevel marketing companies. And, now, through a network of consultants and marketing advisors to nearly 100 different industries, businesses, and professions, I get success education and marketing systems into the hands of more than 1 million business owners every year. All of this gives most of my business activity some meaning greater than just getting money into the bank accounts. From that comes, I think, a different, superior level of creativity, inspiration, and persistence.

Many moons ago, one of the much-made-fun-of Merv Griffin "theme shows" featured a panel of self-made millionaire entrepreneurs: in this instance, Colonel Harlan Sanders of KFC; William Lear, the inventor of the Lear jet; and several others. Merv asked them: "What was your goal—to make money?"

Each guest answered by describing a mission bigger than just making money. Each had a goal, what *Think and Grow Rich* author Napoleon Hill called "a burning desire." Each wanted to *do* something and to *be* someone.

It's interesting that years later, when he was a fabulously wealthy man by most standards (thanks to the sale of his game-show company), Merv Griffin chose to plunge into new, risky businesses rather than just sitting back and enjoying early retirement. He certainly couldn't have been motivated by money itself.

I'm not necessarily saying that you have to have some hidden, ulterior motive or some saintly charitable motive behind your business activities. And I'm not one who feels any guilt about making large amounts of money. But I do find that business owners who are at least as enthusiastic about the values and mission and processes of their businesses as they are about their bank balances do best.

Walt Disney was thrilled when he finally achieved significant financial success, but he was much more committed to his ideals for his theme park than he was to piling up personal wealth. Once, driving home, he noticed an attractive new car in a showroom window and thought to himself: "Gee, I wish I could afford that car." He drove a few more blocks before realizing, "Hey, I *can* afford that car!"

I think you'll find the challenges of successfully crafting and conveying great marketing messages easier and more fun to meet when you are on a magnificent mission!

## It's Time to "Assemble" Your Message

You have undoubtedly had the "joy" of opening a large box and laying out a hundred parts, pieces, screws, and bolts on the floor and trying to assemble it into the beautiful bookcase or computer workstation or whatever was pictured on the outside of the carton. Be honest—how much extra would you pay to get it assembled? (Now there's an idea for a service business: We Put It Together, Inc.)

Well, there you are again, with pieces of a marketing message. Actually, that's where you start. Keeping in mind everything that we've discussed in this chapter, get a large pile of blank 3" × 5" cards and start putting one fact, feature, benefit, promise, offer component, and idea on each card, until you have, over a series of brainstorming sessions, exhausted everything you know about your business and its competitors. Then do your best to prioritize the items, in order of their probable importance to your customers and their contribution to differentiating you from your competition. Through the exercise, you can come to the creation of the best possible USP, a supporting sales story, and one or more related offers.

# Presenting Your Message

Regardless of the target markets you later select and the modifications you make in your message to fit these markets, and regardless of the media mix you use to deliver the presentation of your message, there are some key ideas to keep in mind about making the right presentation.

## The Battle to Communicate

Stew Leonard's famous super-supermarket brought in fresh fish every day, carefully packaged it, and displayed it in the refrigerated cases, clearly and proudly labeled as FRESH FISH. (*Note:* Stew Leonard built one of the largest and most unusual supermarkets and was ahead of his time; many other independents and even chains have since copied much of what he pioneered. You can read about it in Tom Peters's book *In Search of Excellence.*)

Stew Leonard's supermarket had the right message—people who like fish really like fresh fish. Few other supermarkets went to the trouble and expense of bringing in a lot of fresh fish, so the company even had a working USP. It also, incidentally, was getting the right message to the right market; most of Stew Leonard's customers were upscale consumers with the money to buy fresh fish, the time and inclination to prepare a meal with it, and an appreciation for it. Still, something was wrong. It turned out to be a presentation problem.

One of the customers told the people at Stew Leonard's that she wished they had real fresh fish, like the fish at the wharfside fish markets: fish lying there on slabs of ice. So Stew Leonard's people divided the fresh fish that came in each day and presented the same fish two different ways: one, as they had been, cleaned up and nicely packaged; two, unpackaged, on a slab of ice, in a little display unit topped with a sign reading: Fresh Fish Market.

Guess what? Their sales of fresh fish more than doubled. To me, this little story hammers home the idea that it is quite often difficult to communicate successfully.

---

**ULTIMATE MARKETING SECRET WEAPON #2**
**Being Clearly Understood**

---

Lexus and Infiniti, top-luxury cars, were introduced to the market at about the same time, and because Lexus overwhelmingly outsold Infiniti, Infiniti dealers begged the company and its ad agency to "show 'em the car" in the TV commercials. Instead, the company insisted on a Zen-ish series of elegant commercials that never showed the car. A bold experiment, but a bad idea nevertheless.

There *are* notable examples of outrageously clever, intensely creative, excitingly innovative marketing campaigns that have worked well, but if you prefer to put the odds in your favor, you'll pass on this high-risk, long-shot approach and always opt for being clearly understood.

One of the most interesting failure phenomena in advertising is the development of an idea, character, or presentation that is tremendously memorable in itself yet fails to sell the products it represents. Everybody knows about the funny pink bunny with the drum in the battery commercials—but do you know the brand of battery he represents? Surveys show more than half of consumers name the company's competitor! And in a period of five years, while showing off the bunny every way imaginable, that company's market share declined rather than improved.

Another great example of such a misfire is the Taco Bell dog of a few years back. The massive, expensive ad campaign featuring the little stuffed dog wound up selling a lot of little stuffed dogs but reportedly did nothing to improve the chain's market share or sales. The ad campaigns that immediately followed, which refocused attention on the food products, were much more successful.

The confused consumer either does not buy or sometimes buys the wrong product! Bottom line: bend over backward to avoid confusing your customer.

## Presentation Key #1: Be Well Organized

The customer has to be led up five steps to a buying or action decision—to return an order form, redeem a coupon, call for an appointment, come into a store, or buy a product or service—and the five steps are the same for any and every product or service, whether you are marketing to consumers or business-to-business:

**STEP 1:** Awareness of need and/or desire

**STEP 2:** Picking the "thing" that fulfills the need/desire

**STEP 3:** Picking the source for the thing

**STEP 4:** Accepting the source's price/value argument

**STEP 5:** Finding reasons to act now

Sometimes you have to start your presentation at Step 1; other times you get to start on Step 2. A company selling dog food gets to start on Step 2; a company selling dog vitamins has to start on Step 1.

Go back to the Yellow Pages and again turn to the ads in your section. Look at several of them carefully, and ask yourself whether or not, from the top, the headline on down, these ads present their messages according to the organized structure above.

I think you'll agree with me—most do not. Believe me, this is a big mistake. Every presentation of a marketing message via any and every medium should adhere to a safe, proven, effective structure.

Let me give you a couple of great examples of this structure in action:

## Example #1

Some years back I decided to buy a portable fireplace that burns some chemical "logs," gives off heat, glows, replicates the look and the fragrance of a wood fire, but needs no chimney, is safe, and can be moved from the living room to the bedroom with ease. Before I saw this thing in the Hammacher-Schlemmer catalog, I didn't even know such a thing existed or that I needed or wanted one. However, seeing it reminded me that in moving from one house to another, we'd given up a fireplace. I couldn't care less, but my wife at the time really enjoyed the fireplace. (In Phoenix!) So, I instantly became aware of a desire to own a fireplace—in this case, to make my wife happy. I was on Step 1.

I was not about to move to a home with a fireplace, and the home we lived in, which I loved, was not conducive in its design for a built-in, conventional fireplace, nor did I want to incur the expense and bother of having one built. The idea of a portable fireplace was pretty appealing. Okay, up to Step 2.

I wanted one. Where to get it? I'd never seen one anywhere but in this company's catalog. They made it very easy to get—a toll-free call. They even offered to gift wrap the darned thing, so I could give it to my wife as a present. They would deliver it to my door. And they guaranteed I'd be happy with it. Bingo. Step 3.

In this case, Step 4's virtually a must issue, because my thinking has precluded comparison shopping. (By the way, this thing cost $499.00.)

Standing on Step 4, though, the sale breaks down. It's only August, and the next gift-giving occasion is Christmas, so I put the catalog in a pile of stuff to look at later in the year, when I start doing my holiday shopping. The company didn't give me a reason, an incentive, or a reward for ordering immediately.

## Example #2

For many years, I did a considerable amount of consulting work within the chiropractic profession, helping practitioners learn to market their services effectively. I consider the members of this profession my friends, but I must tell you that they remain stubbornly lousy at marketing. Most of them deviate from this organized structure in most of the media they use, yet they need to follow these five steps as badly as any marketer I can think of.

For them, Step 1 has to be creating awareness of the need or the desire: reminding people that they do suffer chronically from, say, head-aches or low back pain or neck stiffness, that they consume frightening quantities of pills, drugs, and alcohol to mute the symptoms, and that deep down inside they desire optimum health and fitness. Chiropractors *cannot* afford to assume that the public is instantly, automatically inter-ested in this.

## ULTIMATE MARKETING SECRET WEAPON #3
### Carefully and Thoroughly Eliminate All Assumptions

Step 2, then, taken only after Step 1, is to present chiropractic care as a viable, effective, accepted, credible, safe, gentle, nonsurgical, nondrug alternative treatment for various problems and ailments. Step 3, taken only after Steps 1 and 2, is the individual chiropractor presenting his USP-empowered marketing message and offer.

Step 4 is handling the issues of fees, costs, and affordability. Here we have taught chiropractors to be creative in offering to accept every imaginable insurance plan, handle all the paperwork, accept major credit cards, even offer installment financing services through finance companies.

Step 5, finally, is pushing the prospective patient over the edge, so he or she picks up the phone right now, calls, makes an appointment, and keeps it.

Fail to walk the customer up those steps, in that order, and you act at your peril.

## Presentation Key #2: Ignite Interest

Please—I don't care if you are marketing Hostess Twinkies, garden hoses, industrial widgets, or any one of a zillion commodities or services that you and everyone you know has accepted as dull and ordinary and mundane, maybe even trivial—there is a way, and you *must* find it, to present that message in a truly interesting way.

## ULTIMATE MARKETING SIN #1
### Being Boring

Some years back, I did some consulting work for a manufacturer of security cameras and video monitoring devices for retail stores. I'm here to tell you that there's nothing inherently fascinating about this.

Still, I knew that I had to *ignite interest* in the storeowner's mind and heart, intellectually and emotionally. I invented a giveaway booklet with this obviously provocative title:

### *HOW TO STEAL YOUR BOSS BLIND!*

Believe me, when a storeowner sees this book, his interest *is* ignited. He eagerly, passionately wants to know what is in the book. Just as an aside, the word "secret" evokes a powerful emotional response in most people. It instantly hits our curiosity button. For some reason, just as cats are bothered by closed doors, we are driven nuts by secrets. We want to know. You can ignite interest easily if you have secrets to divulge.

Consider this: Would you be interested, or do you know somebody who would be interested, in knowing a medical doctor's secret for absolutely, positively suppressing hunger so you can diet, or even skip meals or fast with no hunger pains, no desire for food? If I told you that this doctor's secret had been tested and proven on 10,000 patients, would that make it even more interesting to you?

If at all possible, you should find ways to add drama to your presentations. I've done a lot of scriptwriting and consulting work in the TV infomercial business—you know, those thirty-minute-long commercials that look like TV shows—and, though I haven't worked on them myself, I particularly admire the kind that feature dramatic demonstrations. Maybe you remember one of the classics, in the *Amazing Discoveries* series of infomercials, this one selling car polish, in which they set fire to the hood of the car and poured acid on it! Or Ron Popeil's Food Dehydrator. Or the vacuum cleaner with suction so strong it can pick up a bowling ball. I've had to work on much more difficult infomercials, often featuring interviews and conversations. When the product can be the star, it's an advantage.

You can make the presentation of your marketing message more interesting in many different ways, some depending on the medium being used, including:

1. Before/after photographs
2. Dramatic stories of satisfied customers
3. Shocking statistics
4. Dramatic slogans, headlines, statements
5. Physical demonstration

**Often, it pays to go to extremes to capture attention and ignite interest.** As an example, consider Gold/VIP Member Mitch Carson's work with the Coughlin Group's opening of its new West Coast office. The challenge: establish presence in a new market, where the company was not known, as quickly and efficiently as possible, and immediately generate good sales appointments. Mitch is the leading expert in what I call "object mail": the use of objects in direct mail to ignite interest and response. Working closely with Coughlin's West Coast VP, Kelly Pagett, he created a multistep direct-mail campaign delivered to carefully selected prospects. Letters asking for appointments to provide free risk analysis and discuss fire insurance were sent with:

- A sand pail and shovel
- Toy airplanes
- Rubber duckies
- And finally, boxes of matches

A gift with an appointment, a set of BBQ tools, was also offered. The result: a terrific 46 percent appointment rate!

_____ **Resource!** _____

You can actually see an example from this campaign in the free 12-week Ultimate Marketing Plan Course delivered by e-mail. Sign up at *www.UltimateMarketingPlan.com*. And you can get a lot more information from Mitch at *www.impactproducts.net*.

# Presentation Key #3: Ask for Action

Most marketing-message presentations are too wimpy. They stop short of demanding any action. "Here's our beautiful new car"—but they stop short of: get into a showroom this weekend, take a test drive, and take home a free case of Coke just for test-driving it. "Here's our wonderful new shampoo"—but they stop short of: now go to your phone, dial our toll-free number, and we'll rush you a free sample and $5.00 in discount coupons.

> ## ULTIMATE MARKETING SECRET WEAPON #4
> ### The Guts to Ask for Action Every Time, in Every Presentation

Very early in my selling career, I heard Zig Ziglar say that the difference between being a professional salesperson and a professional visitor is asking for the order. Zig also said: "Timid salespeople have skinny kids." (In case you don't know this already, Zig Ziglar is one of the best-known, most popular motivational speakers and sales trainers in America. His books include *See You at the Top* and *Secrets of Closing the Sale*. For nine consecutive years, I appeared with Zig Ziglar at SUCCESS events in twenty to thirty cities each year, typically addressing audiences of 10,000 to 30,000 people.)

Fortunately, I have always accepted Zig's idea and have never, ever been shy about asking for the action. However, most salespeople, even otherwise very good ones, are held back by this hesitancy, hobbled by some strange love of subtlety.

I spent a full week touring one company's real estate developments, pretending to be a prospective buyer, putting the salespeople through their paces. Almost without exception, all the salespeople did a fine job of establishing rapport, being courteous and friendly, asking smart questions, showing me the communities and the houses. And, almost unanimously, they all stopped way short of asking me to buy.

Four chiropractors joined together and manned a very attractive, professional-appearing booth at a health fair in a busy shopping mall over Labor Day weekend but wound up with no new patients from their efforts. Care to know why? They never asked anybody to book an exam appointment. They smiled, greeted, handed out literature, gave scoliosis exams, checked blood pressure, and answered questions, but they never asked anybody to take any action.

Bill Glazer never fails to ask for action—and he asks a lot. Exhibit #3 is the last page of a mailer sent to his retail stores' customers. Note how many times he asks for action—I've numbered them by hand for you. Six times on one page! This is the way to do it. (To see a copy of this complete mailing, enroll in the free 12-Week Ultimate Marketing Plan Course delivered by e-mail, at *www.UltimateMarketingPlan.com*.)

Again, check the ads in the Yellow Pages. Also look at the ads in a newspaper or the trade magazine related to your business. Isn't it amazing how many stop short of asking you to take any specific action, or, if they do, offer no really good reason, incentive, or reward for doing as they ask? Wimpy. Wimpy. Wimpy.

## Touch Every Base Every Time

You don't have to be a baseball fan to know this rule or, if you prefer, tradition: even when the hitter whacks the ball out of the ballpark and into outer space, it's not a home run on the scoreboard until he goes around the bases—and touches every one. In gym class baseball I was tagged out after hitting a home run and walking the bases but carelessly stepping over second base instead of on it. I've never forgotten that. **The right presentation of the right marketing message touches every base, every time. It assumes nothing. It takes nothing for granted.** It strives for clarity and simplicity and even, many times, brevity—but never, ever achieves those things through shortcuts or skipping bases.

## Exhibit #3

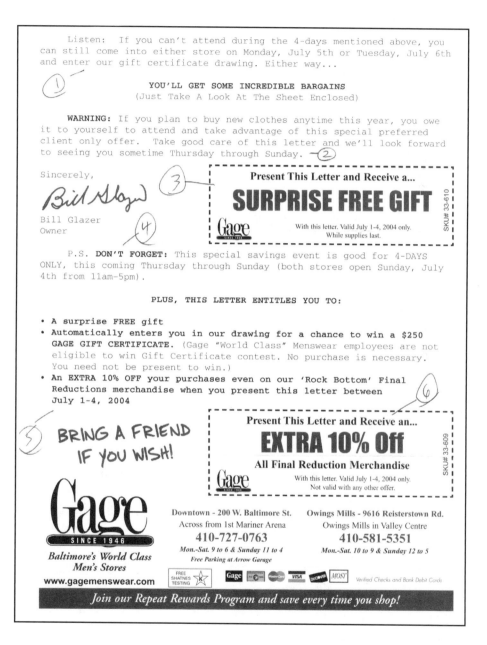

Listen: If you can't attend during the 4-days mentioned above, you can still come into either store on Monday, July 5th or Tuesday, July 6th and enter our gift certificate drawing. Either way...

**YOU'LL GET SOME INCREDIBLE BARGAINS**
(Just Take A Look At The Sheet Enclosed)

**WARNING:** If you plan to buy new clothes anytime this year, you owe it to yourself to attend and take advantage of this special preferred client only offer. Take good care of this letter and we'll look forward to seeing you sometime Thursday through Sunday.

Sincerely,

*Bill Glazer*

Bill Glazer
Owner

**Present This Letter and Receive a...**

# SURPRISE FREE GIFT

**Gage**
SINCE 1946

With this letter. Valid July 1-4, 2004 only.
While supplies last.

SKU# 33-610

**P.S. DON'T FORGET:** This special savings event is good for 4-DAYS ONLY, this coming Thursday through Sunday (both stores open Sunday, July 4th from 11am-5pm).

**PLUS, THIS LETTER ENTITLES YOU TO:**

- A surprise FREE gift
- Automatically enters you in our drawing for a chance to win a $250 **GAGE GIFT CERTIFICATE.** (Gage "World Class" Menswear employees are not eligible to win Gift Certificate contest. No purchase is necessary. You need not be present to win.)
- An **EXTRA 10% OFF** your purchases even on our 'Rock Bottom' Final Reductions merchandise when you present this letter between July 1-4, 2004

*BRING A FRIEND IF YOU WISH!*

**Present This Letter and Receive an...**

# EXTRA 10% Off

**All Final Reduction Merchandise**

**Gage**
SINCE 1946

With this letter. Valid July 1-4, 2004 only.
Not valid with any other offer.

SKU# 33-609

# Gage
SINCE 1946

*Baltimore's World Class
Men's Stores*

www.gagemenswear.com

FREE
SHATNES
TESTING

**Downtown - 200 W. Baltimore St.**
Across from 1st Mariner Arena
**410-727-0763**
*Mon.-Sat. 9 to 6 & Sunday 11 to 4*
*Free Parking at Arrow Garage*

**Owings Mills - 9616 Reisterstown Rd.**
Owings Mills in Valley Centre
**410-581-5351**
*Mon.-Sat. 10 to 9 & Sunday 12 to 5*

Gage [logo] MasterCard VISA DISCOVER MOST *Verified Checks and Bank Debit Cards*

*Join our Repeat Rewards Program and save every time you shop!*

## Which Media Should You Use to Present Your Message?

The list of possible media you might use to present your message is long—from Yellow Pages ads to imprinted snow-scrapers to TV infomercials. There are two fundamental truths about all media. First, while different products, services, businesses, and professions will rank media differently in terms of productivity, efficiency, and appropriateness, you should never unnecessarily or arbitrarily limit your options. You should use all that you can make work. Second, success principles, such as those governing effective presentation of messages, do not change from one medium to the next. A lot of people think they do and act as if they do, but they do not.

There *is* one medium every business should use, and every marketer should learn to use successfully. That is direct mail. That is the subject of the companion to this book, *The Ultimate Sales Letter*, and I urge you to get it, read it, and use it. The sales letter is the most reliable, dependable, practical marketing tool for anyone and everyone. And, to give you one important tip about it right here: of all the direct-mail formats you can choose from, a personalized letter—what we call "A-pile mail"—is the most reliable.

---
### Resource!
---

The leader in personalized mailings and personalized mailing services is Think Ink, and you can request information from them by faxing 714-374-7071 or calling 714-374-7080. You also can enroll free in my 12-Week Ultimate Sales Letter Course, delivered by e-mail, at *www. Ultimate-Sales-Letter.com.*

---

# Picking the Right Targets

MESSAGE

MARKET

MEDIA

There is an old joke about a wife insisting on joining her husband for the first time on his annual deer hunting trip. He stations her at the bottom of the hill and instructs her to fire her gun in the air if she sees any deer, which is very unlikely at that location. He and his buddy then stomp off into the woods. Shortly thereafter, they hear shots and run back through the woods and down the hill to find the wife holding a gun on a very unhappy-looking fellow. "Okay lady," he says, "it's your deer. Can I at least get my saddle off of it?"

Obviously, no matter how well equipped you are with the best gun, bullets, and other hunting equipment, you still won't do very well aiming at the wrong targets.

> ## ULTIMATE MARKETING SIN #2
> ## Wasting Your Weaponry Aiming at the Wrong Targets

My friend and true marketing guru Gary Halbert poses this question: If you were going to open a new hamburger stand in town, what is the one thing you would want most? Many people say that it would be the best hamburgers in town, or a secret sauce, or a great cook, or a commanding name, logo, or character, like Ronald McDonald. But Gary's answer is: a starving crowd. I agree, and our job in Step 3 is to find or develop a starving crowd for your products, services, or business.

## Learning the Lesson

My first introduction to the idea of targeted marketing was so strange that I've never forgotten it, and the more I've learned about the idea, the more I've appreciated that early lesson.

A man with zero training in marketing was running a direct-sales company, selling distributorships for his products at $5,000.00 each. His system was to send out a fairly expensive direct-mail package, get inquiries in return, and then turn those over to staff salespeople called "recruiters," who phoned or visited the prospective distributors and tried to get them to attend a group meeting. As you can see, this process adds up to a sizable investment in each prospect. And, for a while, he was literally mailing to the white pages—to everybody and anybody. He knew this was incredibly inefficient but had no idea how to do it differently. One day, he had what Tom Peters calls "a blinding flash of the obvious": he noticed that a huge majority of his successful distributors had crewcuts. This was in the late 1960s, and crewcuts were supposedly "out." But *his* guys with crewcuts were stubborn individualists, about forty years old, living in small towns, and working in blue-collar jobs—truck drivers, policemen, high-school coaches.

He sent his recruiters out to barbershops all over the state and bought the names, addresses, and telephone numbers of customers who had crewcuts! His success rate with these grade-A prospects was phenomenal.

When he first told me about this, about twenty years ago, I laughed at him. The whole thing sounded ridiculous to me. Maybe it just did to you, too. But now, with 20/20 hindsight, I can tell you that he had stumbled onto the essence of brilliant marketing. He had found one of the three means of picking the right targets: demographics.

## This Is for You, Too

*Every* product, *every* service, *every* business either appeals, or has the potential to appeal, much more strongly to a certain definable group of people than it appeals to *all* people, yet most marketers get to their grade-A prospects only by lucky accident—by throwing out their message to everybody and letting the right people find it. This is like getting a message to your aunt in Pittsburgh by dropping 100,000 copies of your letter out of an airplane as you fly over Pennsylvania. I call this "blind archery." Blindfolded, given an unlimited supply of arrows and some degree of luck, you'll hit the target eventually. And you will hit it once out of every $x$ times you shoot off an arrow. Of course you'll also hit innocent bystanders, bushes, fence posts, stray animals, and everything else around.

Arrows are one thing; dollars are another. Nobody has an unlimited supply of dollars to play with.

You *must* make the commitment to market smarter by picking better targets. Don't say "That's okay for somebody else, but it won't work for my business because. . . ." Don't waste your energy figuring out why this can't be done in your business. Any idiot can come up with that list. You need to find the way it *can* work for you.

# A Few Examples of Targeted Marketing in Action

## Example #1

A fellow in the carpet-cleaning business told me that direct mail never paid off for him. When we investigated the area he had mailed to, we found a very high percentage of renters. More than 70 percent were tenants, not homeowners. "How'd you pick this area, anyway?"

"It was the same Zip Code as my office," he answered.

"Ever drive it, like you were shopping for a home?"

"Nope," he admitted.

"Let's go," I said, and off we went, driving up and down about thirty streets in the area for a couple of hours. We saw many homes in desperate need of repair or paint, poorly maintained lawns, and cars in the driveways and carports five years old or older, some up on jacks being fixed.

"Based on what we've seen outside, who would you expect to see inside these houses?" I asked. 'Nuff said.

The antidote to this direct-mail failure was not fixing the literature; it was simply selecting a better target. The carpet-cleaning guy spent the next few days driving the neighborhoods in various Zip Codes surrounding his office until he found one where the homes shouted pride of ownership.

In the first area, his mailing had pulled less than one-fourth of 1 percent in response. Mailing to residents in the new area, the same mailing pulled more than 2.5 percent.

## Example #2

Several of my clients in very different businesses have discovered the power and leverage of properly targeted marketing.

Larry McEntire's Christian Singles Network helps frustrated American men meet and marry women from dozens of different foreign countries. Historically, he did all of his advertising in general publications, such as *USA Today*. At one of our Gold/VIP coaching group meetings, I asked Larry who his clients were. He initially said "Just about everybody," and named ministers, salespeople, business owners, truck drivers, and doctors. Pushed, he went home and closely examined his records and found that more than 50 percent of all his clients were twice-divorced long-haul truck drivers. More than half! This quickly led to a dramatic change in allocation of ad dollars, focusing on targeted media like truck drivers' magazines; his own "magalog," distributed in free take-one racks placed in truck stops; and other niche media. Profits soared!

In the mortgage business, Scott Tucker identified two different occupational groups that, combined, accounted for about one-third of all his clients. Just like Larry, Scott had been advertising in general media and sending direct mail simply by geographic area, to selected homeowners. And, just like Larry, Scott was able to redirect his ad dollars and better target his direct mail to reach homeowners in these two occupational groups. His return on investment from his ad dollars instantly improved by more than 400 percent.

Darin Garman works with experienced and novice real estate investors purchasing "heartland of America" apartment buildings and commercial properties in Iowa. Prior to some conversations with me, he did all of his advertising and marketing in Iowa, actually in and near his home city. At my urging, he began advertising in national media read by hyperactive investors, such as the *Investors Business Daily* newspaper and *Forbes Magazine*. Clients investing millions of dollars now come from California, New York, and everywhere in between.

## Example #3

Where did Tom Monaghan open up his early Domino's Pizza locations? In college towns, near college campuses. Why? Who do you know who eats more pizza, more often, than college kids? Also, at the time, smoking the funny weed was still immensely popular among college kids and, in case you don't know it, this can make people very, very, very hungry. I have no idea whether or not Tom thought through that—and if he did, I doubt he'd admit it—but he's a bright guy, so you decide for yourself. The point is that, quite literally, he found a starving crowd.

---

### Resource!

For help with direct mail, get the companion to this book, *The Ultimate Sales Letter,* and the free 12-Week Ultimate Sales Letter e-mail course at *www.Ultimate-Sales-Letter.com.*

---

## The Three Best Ways to Target-Market

The first and most commonly used is **geographic targeting,** which is what my friend in the carpet-cleaning business did. Most businesses that need their customers to come to their store or office or that need to schedule appointments and send salespeople out obviously need to restrict the geography of their marketing. They advertise only in the local newspaper or shopper, use coupon decks mailed to their own or adjacent Zip Codes, and direct-mail to those same Zips.

There's nothing wrong and many things right with this. If you've never read Russell Conwell's classic book *Acres of Diamonds* or heard Earl Nightingale's great recorded message, "Greener Pastures," you should; you'll gain new appreciation for the "value" awaiting discovery right in your own backyard.

However, I suggest keeping two things in mind when you are going to select your target markets via geographical considerations:

First, make sure that the apparent nature of the people living there works for you. This is a cheap (in fact, free) and very simplistic look at demographics, but it is nonetheless effective. Do what my carpet-cleaning entrepreneur and I did: drive the neighborhoods. Look around and get a "feel" for the people who live there. You can tell a lot just by driving around. What does the condition of the homes and yards tell you? What kinds of cars predominate? If compacts and sporty cars, young marrieds. If big, bulky sedans and luxury cars, middle-aged. If you see BMWs and the like, upscale professionals. Do you see a lot of tricycles and skateboards, a lot of basketball backboards on the garages?

You may very well be able to choose preferable neighborhoods or Zip Code areas this way. You may also discover things that will cause you to modify your themes, ad copy, and offers.

My second tip is, once you find a geographic target market that works for you, work it to death. Dominate it. People in the real estate business use the term "farming." When a real estate agent farms an area, he strives to become its best-known and loved agent. He mails to every homeowner in the area, goes around door-to-door and introduces himself, distributes a monthly newsletter, sends holiday greeting cards, even gets creatively involved with the community: driving through and giving away free pumpkins at Halloween, sponsoring a neighborhood block party and swap meet, and so on. It's a lot of work, but it's smart work. If you get adept at using media, particularly direct mail, you can replace much or even all of the manual labor stuff.

There's no reason why any retail or service business can't follow this example. If I had a florist shop, a restaurant, or a car wash, I could do exactly the same thing in a targeted residential or business neighborhood. I could frequently mail to everybody. I could take an hour each day and go out and personally introduce myself to the neighbors. I could send holiday greetings. I could throw a party. I could lead a charitable effort in the area for the Muscular Dystrophy Association or some other worthwhile group.

A second selection method has to do with **demographics.** Demographics are the statistical, behavioral, and even psychological things given groups of people have in common. Demographic selection can be as simple as targeting a preferred age group or as complex as targeting women age 35 to 45 who have careers, read both *Working Woman* and

*Cosmopolitan,* carry the American Express card, travel by air at least three times a year, and buy clothes by mail order.

Every medium has, and can provide, detailed demographic information about its readers, listeners, viewers, or customers. While some media's data is more reliable than others, most are pretty accurate—the media need this same data to make good editorial, programming, or product selections. You can and should take this information very seriously when making media decisions.

If you're renting mailing lists, the same kind of data is available for most lists. More significantly, you can "merge-purge" two or more lists together to get exactly the prospective customers you want. A good list broker can help. It can be quite costly to do sophisticated merge-purges, but even so it's usually a bargain compared to the costly waste of playing "blind archery" with direct mail.

Think again about my friend in the carpet-cleaning business. After choosing one or several Zip Code areas based on his drive-by observations, he could get even pickier. He might make the logical assumption that people in certain income brackets are better prospects than are others. Folks with household incomes of, say, less than $30,000.00 a year might find money tight and choose to go through the agony of shampooing their own carpets to save money.

Because he accepts VISA and MasterCard, he might prefer to mail only to people who have those credit cards, and because families get their carpets dirtier more often, he might want to skip mailing to single people.

So he sits down with his list broker and says: "In these Zips, I want married homeowners with kids, with a household income of $30,000.00 and up, who have MasterCards or VISA cards." Using lists derived from the census, credit card holder lists, property ownership records, and other readily available sources, the broker can deliver that exact list.

Incidentally, it can be helpful to collect demographic data about your present customers. If you find certain biases or commonalities in your present customers, you may be able to use them in your criteria for future targeting.

**The third way to target market is by affinity or association.** I like this approach and use it a great deal for myself and my clients.

Let me give you a personal example: I've been a member of the National Speakers Association, one of two trade associations for lecturers and seminar leaders, since 1978. I have gone out of my way to be visible in the association, through a variety of means, and I'd guess my "name recognition" hits about 70 to 80 percent of the total membership, about 4,000 people. These 4,000 people and I have much in common: first, obviously, I know them and, more importantly, they know me. I can call attention to our affinity by addressing them as "colleagues" and "fellow members." We share the same business activities, experiences, concerns, and problems. Because I am a known, respected success in this business, the members are interested in what I have to say and in whatever I recommend.

In approximately twenty years, I have sold millions of dollars of goods and services to this very small market. In some years, as much as one-third of my income has been derived from this very small market. I am occasionally able to reap pure passive income simply from licensing my endorsement of someone else's product or service, which is being offered to this very small market.

Geographically, these people are scattered all over the United States, Canada, and several foreign countries. Demographically, they have few, if any, dominant commonalities. They are men, women, young, old, fat, thin, conservative, liberal, rich, poor, married, single, with families, without families. But they are still a perfect target market for me purely because of our mutual association. Because of affinity.

Here is evidence of how well affinity works for me with this target market: Just as I was doing revisions and updating the second edition of this book, I was in the midst of a direct-mail campaign to this list for a new product and had brought in $226,400.00. Just a year ago, I conducted a simple direct-mail campaign for another, new information product to this group and did nearly $600,000.00 in sales. All from only about 4,000 people.

Many other businesspeople can apply this same principle to the trade or professional associations they belong to or to the local chamber of commerce, Toastmasters, Jaycees, other business and civic groups, church groups, PTAs—whatever they belong to. I encourage chiropractors and dentists I consult with, for example, to get out of their offices at least eight hours a week to join and actively participate in a number of these associative target markets. Then, instead of advertising to a neighborhood, they can advertise to their fellow members. Instead of farming a community, they can farm a fraternity.

## ULTIMATE MARKETING SECRET WEAPON #5
## Tailoring and Delivering Your Message to the Right Target

I find the pizza wars endlessly interesting. Domino's took the industry by storm by focusing on delivery. Another company has taken a very different tack and is enjoying great success by targeting a very specific demographic group. Pistol Pete's Pizza, with stores in several states here in the Southwest, very clearly aims its products, prices, restaurant environments, and advertising at families.

Each location features a working merry-go-round and lots of other games for the kids. The TV commercials use a happy cowboy character who urges families to c'mon in and have fun. Their pricing is low-end, so the family can be fed without breaking the piggy bank. It's worth noting that Pistol Pete's does *not* bother trying to convince anybody it has the best pizza. If you see the chain's commercials and are taking a date to a movie, Pistol Pete's is *not* the place you'll stop at afterward. This chain has locked its sights on a very specific, identifiable, identified starving crowd. Those people that the chain is after know it's for them.

In Las Vegas, for many years, most casino-hotels aggressively pursued the business of the "high rollers." An acquaintance of mine has the title "Casino Host" at one of the biggest hotels on the Strip; he's actually a recruiter who goes to other hotels, to parties in Beverly Hills and New York where the rich gather, even to Japan, to invite and inveigle high rollers to come to the hotel he represents. Then, when they do, they are his honored and privileged guests, with complimentary rooms, meals, shows, airfare, and limousines. Every big casino operation has such people. One high roller I know described Las Vegas as "the home of the $10,000.00 free drink."

Bob Stupak, the successful entrepreneur I mentioned earlier, ignored this market almost entirely. Nothing he did was targeted at the high roller. To the contrary, his market was middle-income, middle-America, mom 'n' pop, everyday folks, many of them first-time visitors to "Glitter City." While the others chased the Saks customer, Bob preferred Sears. If the other hotels got people with Cadillacs, Mercedes, and even Rolls-Royces in their garages, Bob attracted the people with three-year-old station wagons. While the other hotels pursued the country-club crowd, Bob recruited at the bowling alleys. For a handful of recent years, Las Vegas refocused its sights on families, with many casino resorts creating Disneyesque, family-friendly environments, and the city briefly surpassed Orlando as the #1 vacation destination. However, in recent years, the realization set in that adult customers were more reliable and valuable, so Vegas has shifted back more to its old image as "Sin City," with nightclubs featuring scantily clad dancers, more "skin" shows, and the suggestive ad slogan: "What happens in Vegas, stays in Vegas."

This city's business leaders are constantly, closely analyzing their different markets and constituencies, and tailoring and delivering different marketing messages to different target markets. You can gain a great deal from emulating their examples.

# Proving Your Case

The American public has been lied to so much by so many that we no longer trust anybody. In fact, research I've been privy to, thanks to the Guthy-Renker Corporation's expensive consumer focus groups, shows that a first instinct is to passionately distrust. Make no mistake about it: This is the Age of Skepticism.

There is an old joke—told to me by a very cynical businessman— about the father who puts his three-year-old son up on the fireplace mantel and holds out his hands and urges him to jump. "I'll catch you," he promises. After much coaxing and coercion, the kid jumps toward Daddy, who steps back and lets him crash to the floor. He then leans over the wailing youngster and says: "You've just learned your first great lesson of life—don't trust anybody."

The consumer and the business customers, your prospective customer or client, has been coerced off the mantel and allowed to crash to the floor one too many times. Lucy has pulled the football away at the last minute one time too many, and Charlie Brown won't play anymore.

> **ULTIMATE MARKETING SECRET WEAPON #6**
> **Marketing Messages Developed with the Understanding That Recipients Will Be Stubbornly Reluctant to Believe Them**

A client came to me recently with a most interesting marketing problem: a truly irresistible offer that didn't work. His product is a certificate good for at least $500.00 worth of travel, including two nights in any one of several dozen good hotels scattered around the country—a $400.00 discount. You can take a three-day cruise for just $99.00 per person, and take advantage of several other offers. He sells these certificates to various businesses to use as premiums and incentives, at only five cents each—that's right!—five cents each! The ultimate recipient of the certificate needs only to pay a $10.00 processing fee to use it, and my client has made that ridiculously easy: call a 900 number, hear a message about a trip and tour offers, and a $10.00 charge appears on your telephone bill.

Unfortunately, he's been having a tough time getting businesses to buy and use these things. And he's finding that a shockingly small percentage of the people who get them make the call to redeem them. How can this be? "Why," he asked, "doesn't this work better than it does?"

By now, of course, the answer is obvious, isn't it? The darned offer is just too good to be true. People don't believe it.

Today, if you make any kind of a free or big-discount offer, the consumer says to himself or herself, "Who's he kidding? Nothing's free. There's got to be a catch here somewhere." Or: "Fifty percent off, my eye! All they've done is jacked up the price so they can mark it back down. It's all baloney."

My research indicates that people don't even believe guarantees. They say: "Yeah, just try to get your money back. You've got to bring it back still wrapped in the original plastic, fill out a sixteen-part form, stand in line for three hours, and scream and yell and threaten their lives." I believe you should use guarantees, and even lean heavily on them. But you have to go to extremes to make people believe them.

If you use testimonials—and I'm going to tell you that you should—people will say: "I'll bet those are actors" or "I'll bet they're just made up" or "I'll bet they paid those people to say those things."

## So, How Do We Prove Our Case?

I sat, as an uninvolved observer, in the giant, lavishly decorated law firm conference room and watched and listened as one of this country's most famous trial attorneys conducted his pretrial conference with his associates, investigators, researchers, and paralegals. Each person summarized his or her work and each gave an opinion on the probable outcome.

One young attorney assured the boss, "I think you've got enough evidence to win this thing."

The boss came unglued. He slammed his hands down on the table and rocked the room. He lunged across the table, grabbed the young guy by his Brooks Brothers lapels, yanked him up, faced him nose-tip to nose-tip and bellowed loud enough to be heard on the opposite coast: *"Do not ever send me into a courtroom to face a jury with just enough evidence."* He paused, dropped the shocked attorney back into his chair, walked to the end of the room, and wrote these words on the blackboard:

## *PREPONDERANCE OF PROOF*

Webster defines "preponderance" as a superiority in weight, power, importance, strength, or quantity. *Roget's Thesaurus* suggests these synonyms: majority, plurality, advantage, supremacy, maximum, lion's share, excess, surplus, redundancy, and domination. I suggest that you want all that and more when you present your case to the customer.

# How to Go from Zero to Maximum Credibility

If we wanted an example of an industry with near-zero credibility, we need look no further than the people and businesses behind the automobile sitting outside in the driveway. Automobile salespeople are distrusted by everybody.

My own informal—but I think fairly accurate—survey shows that those who are ranked at the very bottom of the credibility ladder by the public are medical doctors; then lawyers; then, still worse, politicians; then, worst of all, car salesmen. And, quite frankly, in my opinion, they deserve this. If any other industry played the pricing games that the car dealers get away with, everybody would be in jail. Typically, people in the automobile business use artificial retail prices to create phony discounts, they advertise stripped models to play bait-and-switch, they use deceptive sales practices, they bully their customers, they sell grossly overpriced insurance add-ons, and they are notorious for lousy service after the sale. Both the Federal Trade Commission and the attorneys general of this country should be ashamed of themselves for permitting this stuff to continue.

However, there are good, honest, reputable exceptions to this rule.

The most honest, and, I think, not coincidentally, the most successful automobile salesman I've ever known is Bill Glazner at Sanderson Ford in Phoenix. (Not to be confused with Bill Glazer, who is featured frequently throughout this book and is publisher of my *No B.S. Marketing Letter*, president of Glazer-Kennedy Inner Circle, and president of his own marketing advice business serving retailers. They are not the same person, and are not related.) He managed to attain maximum credibility in a business that, overall, has no credibility—a tough task, but a great marketing lesson.

For years, I bought all of my cars from Bill. Here was the experience, consistent every time: When you went to buy a car from Bill, like most anywhere else, you went out on the lot and looked at cars, kicked tires, maybe test-drove a couple. Eventually you were led down the hall where the long row of salesmen's cubicles were located. These are pretty much the same everywhere. You've been in more than one. The walls are ticky-tacky plywood partitions, and in each cubicle there's a basic military-issue gray or green metal desk. There are two turquoise or orange plastic stackable chairs for the customers. And that is it.

Bill's cubicle was the same as the others you've seen—except for one little detail. Floor to ceiling, side to side, every square inch of wall space was covered with instant snapshots of Bill's customers, proudly posed next to their new cars, with their names and dates of purchase written on them. I never counted the photos, but the quantity was overwhelming. Then, if you looked a little closer, you would pick up two patterns in the arrangement of the snapshots. First, the relationship pattern. For example, next to the picture of me with my Lincoln, you would have seen the photo of my wife with her Taurus, my parents with their Mercury, my brother with his pickup truck, my business partner with his Lincoln, his wife with her Probe, his sales manager with his Tempo, and one of his office managers with his Focus. Also, you would have noted a historical pattern. Not just me with my current Lincoln, but backwards chronologically to me with the Lincoln before that. In some cases, there were five, even six such photos: the customer with his new car, the same customer with the car he bought in 2000, again with the car he bought in 1996, again with the car he bought in 1992.

Now I'm going to tell you something that is almost unbelievable. I've gone there with my ex-wife, with business associates, and with friends while they bought cars from Bill and I have watched, in every case, as Bill figured up the price, wrote it on the contract, and quoted the price and payment amounts, and heard the customers say, "Fine." I've watched them sign on the dotted line without even once haggling over price. In the car business!

In the weight-loss business, one very successful sales representative for diet products carries a sales tool with her everywhere she goes: a photo blown up into a life-size poster of herself, fifty-four pounds heavier than she is today. She unrolls the poster and stands next to it, and the sale is made.

Some thirty-five years ago, I was at an Amway Rally where the guest speakers were Charlie and Else Marsh, enormously successful distributors. The experience stuck in my mind so, that I'm still using it as an example today. You need to understand that Amway uses a multilevel marketing system, where distributors recruit others, who recruit others, and so on, and earn overrides on the performance of everybody "down line" from them and those they recruit. Distributors need to be convinced that the plan really works and that they can, in fact, build a large organization and income by recruiting.

Charlie pulled a half-dozen volunteers out of the audience up onto the auditorium's stage, and they started at one end of the stage and unfolded a huge, five-foot-high and fifty-foot-wide hunk of posterboard with Charlie's immense distributor organization diagrammed out, with each distributor's name and home city listed next to the little circle that represented each person. The thousands and thousands of connected circles all emanated from about fifteen people Charlie had personally recruited into the business. He said, "If you know fifteen people, you can do this, too."

When you walk into my chiropractor's office, you'll see one wall almost entirely covered with instant snapshots of the practitioner standing next to each smiling, happy patient. You see, these pictures are *instantly convincing*.

## ULTIMATE MARKETING SECRET WEAPON #7
### Pictures That Prove Your Case

Let me tell you something funny. For dozens of years, Bill Glazner out-performed his sales colleagues at Sanderson Ford month after month, year after year—yet he was the only salesman there with photographs up on his cubicle walls. In the diet products company that the lady with the life-size "before" poster sells for, there are more than 15,000 representatives, but as far as I know, only one has a poster of her overweight former self.

The night I saw Charlie Marsh unroll his organizational chart, there were at least *500* Amway distributors in the audience, many of whom I knew. To the best of my knowledge, nobody "stole" Charlie's idea.

From 1983 to 1987, I built the largest integrated seminar and publishing firm exclusively teaching marketing to chiropractors and dentists, and, in one way or another, I told all of these stories to at least 15,000 doctors during those years. I'm still telling these same stories to the doctors. Yet, to the best of my knowledge, there's only one with a photo on the wall.

Maybe all of that is a comment on my effectiveness. I hope not. I think not. Instead, I think it is simply a reflection of the vast majority's interest in improving, but only if doing so requires no change, discomfort, or initiative. That's why, in every field, a few out-earn the huge "mediocre majority" by giant margins.

## Who Says So?

What others say about you, your company, your products, and your services is infinitely more credible than anything you can say on your own behalf. When you make a statement, it's a claim. When your satisfied customer makes the same statement about you, that's a *fact*.

I am here to tell you that you cannot overuse testimonials.

Some businesses, notably the weight-loss industry, do an outstanding job of getting and using good testimonials—check out advertising by Weight

Watchers, or TV infomercials like Guthy-Renker's infomercials for Proactiv acne products or Victoria Principal skin care. During the time I was writing the first edition of this book, Citibank was running a very effective series of TV commercials for its VISA card, featuring real people telling of the help they got from Citibank when they lost their cards or when they needed additional credit. Another testimonial-driven TV campaign of a very similar nature had Lee Iacocca personally interviewing car accident victims saved by Chrysler's air bags. What these people said was believable. It had the obvious ring of truth. In Citibank's case, it made the incredible credible, the unbelievable believable; that a bank really cares about its customers and will quickly respond to their special needs and problems, anytime, twenty-four hours a day. This strategy will never go out of style, never run out of gas.

### —————————— Resource! ——————————

There's more information about selling with testimonials, and a terrific example of using emotional testimonial stories for a very un-emotional product, in my book *No B.S. Sales Success* (information at *www.nobsbooks.com*).

But now I'm going to let you in on a "secret." As common and well-proven as testimonial use is, the absence or underuse of testimonials remains *the* number one marketing error I see repeated most frequently. For example, in many of my audiocassette courses I give out "Critique Coupons" that entitle people to send in their ads, brochures, sales letters, or other marketing materials for my critique. Some months I handle hundreds of these. I'd guess that I responded to at least a few thousand last year alone.

They come from every imaginable kind of business; from the butchers, bakers, and candlestick makers of the world; from marketing novices, but also from people who ought to know the basics. Without question, the suggestion I send back to these folks so frequently I get sick of saying it is:

*"Hey, where are your testimonials?"*

I can promise you this: If you get nothing else out of this entire book but the inspiration to collect and heavily use as many good testimonials as you can possibly get, you'll have a strong competitive advantage from that alone.

Currently, my Gold/VIP Member Dr. Barry Lycka has a cosmetic surgery practice and is a consultant to a separate spa business, the Corona Rejuvenation Center and Spa, both in Edmonton, Canada. And he is a consultant and coach to cosmetic surgeons throughout the world. Dr. Lycka has really embraced this idea. At the Corona Spa, each consultation room includes a huge book with hundreds of testimonials from happy patients. Unfortunately, Canadian law prohibits use of the same kind of testimonial presentations for the cosmetic surgery practice; fortunately, U.S. doctors are free to use testimonials—and should! Dr. Charles Martin employs an identical strategy at his cosmetic dentistry practice and teaches hundreds of dentists to use testimonials in every step of their practice marketing process. Doctors seem to "get this" easier than do other types of business owners, yet *every* type of business should heavily utilize testimonials.

---

### Resource!

You can see some of Dr. Martin's testimonial-driven advertising and marketing at *www.martin-method-dentistry.com*, and get more information at *www.AffluentPracticeSystems.com*. You can see Dr. Lycka's testimonial-driven marketing and get more information at *www.cosmeticsx.com*.

---

## What Is a Good Testimonial?

For starters, think of a testimonial as a pair of verbal "snapshots." The first is the "Before" picture—the problem or the skepticism; the second is the "After" picture—the positive result, the pleasant surprise, the solution.

"I was fat, lonely, frightened, poor, unhappy, skeptical, etc.—now, thanks to XYZ, I'm thin, popular, confident, rich, happy, and a believer!"

Second, view testimonials as strategic weapons. I suggest making two lists; one of every claim, feature, benefit, and fact about what you're marketing that you want to substantiate; second, every doubt, fear, or question that might exist in your prospective customer's mind. Then collect and use testimonials that specifically substantiate the claims that eliminate the doubts.

## A Few Examples

A cafeteria wants to attract new customers. The owners are eager to emphasize the variety of foods they offer and the fact that, unlike some cafeterias, they keep their food hot and fresh. The owners also know there are a great many people who would never dream of coming to a cafeteria. They position these testimonials against that initial negative image:

> I haven't eaten in a cafeteria since high school, but I'm sure glad a friend brought me here—I'm really surprised at the tremendous variety that's offered. Finally there's someplace I can take the whole family for dinner and make everybody happy.

> I've always thought that cafeteria food sat around on hot plates and got soggy. Maybe that is true elsewhere, but everything here is piping hot, fresh, and, well, really good.

A dentist "made hay" with this great testimonial:

> I avoided dental care I knew I needed for almost a year because I didn't want the pain. I just couldn't stand the thought of going to the dentist. But I've got to say that Dr. Welmer and his staff were just terrific! They were patient and understanding. And things sure have changed since the last time I went to a dentist. Dr. Welmer's got the newest technology so the treatment was virtually pain-free. I was amazed.

And this powerful testimonial for a lawn service:

I'm busy, I travel a lot on business, and I hate taking care of my lawn. It always needed to be cut. Plants died. I tried different lawn care guys—you know, the guys with beat-up old pickup trucks who come around and hang Xeroxed flyers on your door, then never show up when they're supposed to. When the representative of Lawn Technicians knocked on my door and I agreed to use them, I was prepared for another aggravating disappointment. Now, three months later, I'm telling everybody I know to use Lawn Technicians. They've turned lawn care into a profession.

Some business owners incorrectly feel that customer testimonials aren't important for "ordinary" businesses, but I differ. Here, in Exhibit #4, is a successful example from Bill Glazer: a marketing piece for his menswear stores that is dominated by testimonials.

## The Expanded Testimonial

In print advertising, you'll usually see short testimonials, two or three sentences long. On TV and radio, they're usually a few seconds, except in thirty-minute-long infomercials, where each testimonial may run for a couple of minutes. Even though short is the norm, there may be cases in which you'll want to use an expanded testimonial.

Another use of the expanded testimonial is in article form. Some magazines, especially trade magazines, have an unwritten policy of giving advertisers editorial space without added cost along with the ad space. This is common in the business opportunity field, with magazines such as *Spare Time* and *Moneymaking Opportunities*. Reprinted as Exhibit #5 (page 56) is an "article" I wrote for a client, U.S. Gold Chain, and furnished to the magazine. To the reader, it seems like an article. For the client/advertiser, it's really an extended testimonial.

**Exhibit #4**

**Exhibit #5**

# Family Discovers Amazing Part Time Profits

Carolyn and Bob Harniss of Barberton, Ohio had good jobs — he managed an office supply warehouse store and she was a receptionist at an insurance company. After four years of marriage, they were living well but not extravagantly, saving some money but still a long way away from having the money needed for a down payment on a new home.

One day, Carolyn found an ad of U.S. Gold Chain in *Money Making Opportunities Magazine*. This company's "Gold By The Inch" business opportunity sounded good to her so she tore out the ad and showed it to her husband. She says, "I told Bob that everyone loves gold jewelry. I think it would be easy to sell this gold in lots of different ways. Maybe we could make enough money with this business to buy a new home."

Although Bob was a little skeptical about the whole idea, they sent for the catalog and then, after looking it over, sent for the $399.00 Starter Kit. "Frankly, I went along at Carolyn's insistence," Bob admits. "I figured if worst came to worst, we could sell enough of the chains to friends and people we knew to get our money back and then give the rest away as gifts."

When the Starter Kit arrived a few days later, Bob changed his mind. "I was surprised to find everything needed to operate this as a real business. There was even a video tape that showed us exactly how to make the chain and how easy it is to sell it." In the Starter Kit, U.S. Gold Chain provides 12 spools of the most popular styles of beautiful gold-layered chains, the clasps and tools to create the jewelry on the spot, a large, attention-getting sign plus Manufacturers Lifetime Guarantee Certificates for the customers! The kit, which costs only $399.00, has enough inventory in it to produce over $3,000 in profits for the Distributor.

On the first weekend after receiving the Starter Kit, Carolyn and Bob went out to a swap meet in their area. Carolyn recalls, "We were just amazed at the interest that people had in Gold By The Inch. There was a crowd of people around our booth from midmorning to the end of the day."

"My fingers were actually a little sore from making the chains," Bob says, "but I didn't care. We sold over $450 worth of chains that weekend. Because of the huge markup on Gold By The Inch, that represented about $400 in clear profits for us. About $200 a day! We had recovered our entire investment and still had a large inventory of chains to sell."

Bob and Carolyn had dinner on Sunday with her parents and her father commented that he had never heard of a business you could start that easily and recover your start-up costs so quickly. He then called a friend who owned a greeting card store in a local shopping mall and arranged a meeting between Carolyn and Bob with this man. That led to them putting a Gold By The Inch set-up in the front of that store and the following weekend, they sold nearly $1,000 worth of chains. When Carolyn's father saw how well they did, he had to get involved. Now they have two and sometimes three locations operating almost every weekend. Carolyn explains, "Bob, I, my Dad and sometimes my younger brother work the locations and share the profits."

"We've been Gold By The Inch distributors for almost a year and we've put over $11,000 into the savings account for the down-payment on our house. We're going to buy our new home early next year," says Bob. In the meantime, Carolyn has quit her job and is devoting her time to managing and expanding the business. Both Carolyn and Bob agree that this has been the best move they have ever made!

Gold By The Inch distributors did over $20,000,000 worth of business last year and they have only scratched the surface of the demand for gold chains. There is still a ground floor opportunity open with U.S. Gold Chain, a major force in the quality costume jewelry field.

You can receive a free information kit including a beautiful full color catalog and wholesale price list. Just write to U.S. Gold Chain Mfg. Co., Dept. MM-1, 11460 N. Cave Creek Rd., Phoenix, AZ 85020. If you would like a video tape that shows everything about the business, include a $10.00 refundable deposit when you write. Return the video within 30 days or place an order and your $10.00 will be refunded.

Another fine example of an expanded testimonial comes from one of my Platinum Inner Circle Members and private clients, Rory Fatt of Restaurant Marketing Systems. Shown as Exhibit #6 (page 58) is one of many different full-page ads he runs in restaurant industry trade journals, each ad featuring one of his successful clients' stories. Rory writes some of these ads himself, I write some of them, and they have proven to out-perform ads that are directly about him and his company by a big margin. These "human interest ads" are superior for many reasons. They are more believable, because a real person, industry peer, someone the reader can identify with, is telling his story. The ads feature the person's photograph and are, in part or whole, written in first person.

—————————————— **Resource!** ——————————————

To learn more about Rory Fatt's marketing of his business, or about the phenomenally successful marketing he provides to restaurant owners, visit *www.roryfatt.com.*

# Exhibit #6

*Beat the pants off the National Chains*

## John Brashear Skyrockets His Restaurant's Sales With Secret He Learned In Two Hours

*Don't Laugh It Really Did Happen And More Importantly It Could Happen To You!!!!*
*Free Report Reveals How You Can Double Your Restaurant's Profits in 119 Days or Less...*

**Conway, Arkansas**

My name is John Brashear and I live in a town that has a population of about 40,000 people. For years I was the number one restaurant until 1992 when I started seeing the national chains move in. Quite frankly, I did not know how to compete with them.

It was a disastrous 2 to 3 years and I was fighting ever since then to try to hold on to my market share. As soon as I felt I got it going my way again, three or four more national chains came into town and, before I knew it, there were so many restaurant seats it was hard to compete.

I tried every imaginable type of advertising and promotion with no success. Comparing one month against the same month of the previous year, I had declining sales ranging from as good as a negative 2% to almost 9%. We were down, down, down.

I am part of a regional franchise system but I decided I needed to take control of my marketing myself. I noticed an article in one of the trade publications I got. I found it hard to believe the promises it made. But, I felt I didn't have anything to lose so I called in for the free report.

At first I was skeptical, but I decided I didn't have anything to lose. My test only cost $14.16. I was amazed by the results so I expanded it. The next time I did it cost me $134.50 and it generated $2015.95 and 364 new customers. I did it again and it made me $10,801.04! Since I learned this secret sales are up consistently every month and the opportunity to expand this is enormous. The best part is I'm seeing the biggest increase in the bottom line.

All this only took a few hours to learn. Wow, I mean, I've never ever, ever, in the 23 years I have been in the restaurant business have I been I able to actually measure such a result from my marketing.

Now I look forward to getting up in the morning because I'm excited again. Here's a couple of other things I've learned since learning that little secret.

• Two ways to get people to flock to your restaurant that cost you nothing.

• How to hire and retain a superstar staff

• How to double profits on your existing customers.

• How to get free publicity for your restaurant in the local media.

• How to beat the cheapest price restaurants & avoid price competition altogether

*How did John Brashear go from battling the National Chains to skyrocketing his sales in 12 months? Call 1-800-562-5681 to find out.*

• How to find out who my best customers are and how to get more just like them

• How to drive the national chains crazy

• How not to make the big mistake that costs restaurant owners thousands of dollars a year

• How to get your customers excited about referring your restaurant to your friends and business associates.

• How to get 54.6% of the people who see one of my ads to come to my restaurant.

• Why boring, traditional advertising is a waste, how to avoid using it forever and how to quit being a victim of advertising sales reps.

As I was writing this I was closing the blinds in my office to the windows that overlook my parking lot. As I was looking over my parking lot that holds 110 cars, there were some 50 to 60 customers walking toward my restaurant almost in sequence. I could not believe it. It was a sight to behold. The next morning I learned we had sales 2.5 times a normal Thursday. The thrill is back!!!!!!!

I wrote this without any compensation. Because one, its time to fight back against these nationals chains, two I have suffered along with you before finding this secret and it's only fair that I share it. That's why my head office <u>insisted</u> I speak at three regional franchise meetings and they're already talking to me about speaking at our national convention next spring. They <u>know</u> I am onto something big and three I promised the person who taught me this secret that I would tell my story if it worked. Telling my story is just my part of the bargain.

Please be reasonable about this: I have a restaurant to run and a life of my own, so don't try to track me down and call me.

What more do I need to say? You can find out all you want to know without spending even one cent of your money. Call the toll free phone number below like I did, listen to the free recorded message, and then leave your name and address, and you'll get a complete 20 page report: "How To Double Your Restaurant's Profit's In 119 Days Or Less", a collection of fascinating success stories like mine, plus a terrific audio cassette tape, all free.

Unless you are already taking all the money you want out of your restaurant... already have zero worries about keeping a steady flow of good new customers coming....and are already living a successful entrepreneur's lifestyle... why wouldn't you call and get this giant, FREE package of information?

Over 1028 restaurant owners throughout the US, Canada and Australia just like me have learned this secret and given their restaurant and incomes a makeover. Can 1028 people all be wrong? Why not investigate what so many of us have already discovered—how this secret can work in your restaurant too. Oh, and it doesn't matter whether you're suffering or doing okay, or even doing well but would like to do better, or want to work less, make more and enjoy it more. This secret works in all types of situations. How do I know? Because I've talked to many other people who have learned this secret and it's being used in big cities, small towns and everything in-between all over the country.

Don't let anyone get in the way of what you want out of your business, and out of life. Don't let pride get in your way either. It's easy to confuse effort with results. Even if you have lots of experience in this industry it's very dangerous to close your eyes to new ideas. To check out what I have said is FREE doesn't it just make good sense to look into it?

Here's all you have to do: Just pick up the phone and dial toll free 24 hours **1-800-562-5681.** It's a free call. You will NOT be connected to any kind of pushy salesman—in fact, you'll hear a brief recorded message, then you can leave your name and address on the voice mail and you'll get the information in the mail. Nobody's ever going to call and bug you! What are you waiting for?

©2001 RMS a divison of Simple Salmon North America Inc.

## Real-People Versus Celebrity Testimonials

Real-people testimonials are, in my opinion, a mandatory component of a solid marketing message. These typically come from your satisfied customers. When using a number of these testimonials in one message, you want to try to cover as many claim-benefit bases and as many demographic bases as possible.

If marketing to a demographically diverse group of consumers, you need testimonials from whites, blacks, Asians, and Hispanics; men, women, married, and single people; and the old, the middle-aged, and the young.

If you're doing business-to-business marketing, the bases you might want to cover include small companies, medium-sized companies, and big companies—as well as retailers, wholesalers, manufacturers, and service businesses. Of course, if you're aiming at a much more narrow, specific target market, then you can match your testimonial sources to it.

I consider it fair to coach and coax in order to get the testimonial comments you want, but unfair, and often also woefully ineffective, to put words in the mouths of people providing testimony.

Celebrity testimonials can be effective, but they also can be tricky. If your product or service is used or your business patronized by a known personality, such as an athlete or entertainer, you can capitalize on it. Sometimes even an endorsement of your general industry is useful. Some years back, Roger Craig and Joe Montana, both then playing for the San Francisco 49ers football team, stated that they relied on chiropractors to keep them healthy. I said then, and I'll still say it today: any chiropractor who would not think to use this fact to market to patients is just plain dumb.

When marketing on a national scale, you need nationally known celebrities, but when marketing locally, a local personality may prove nearly equal in impact but is usually a lot easier and less costly to get.

Two different chains of weight-loss clinics use the identical strategy of paying local radio disc jockeys and talk-show hosts to lose weight in their clinics, then serve as spokespersons in the commercials, giving personal testimony. This has proven extraordinarily effective for both companies.

In our market, I've seen a restaurant using the endorsement of a very popular former governor, car dealers using football players, a bank using a football coach, and a chiropractor using a female rodeo star.

You should not just assume that your local business cannot afford a national celebrity. My Gold/VIP Member Scott Tucker, a mortgage broker in Chicago primarily marketing to "blue collar" clients, secured the services of the still immensely popular former Chicago Bears player William "the Refrigerator" Perry. A photograph of the Fridge with Scott and his dog Boomer is now featured in Scott's mailings. The photo is printed on the back with an endorsement message from the Fridge, using a type font made from the Fridge's actual handwriting. The message is even personalized to each recipient!

Scott says people are very reluctant to throw these photos out—in fact, they put them up on the 'fridge! The fact that people do this has improved immediate response to his mailings, but he's also noticed additional response from people who call weeks, even months after receiving a mailing and tell him it's because they kept that photo around the house. Perry also appears in a video clip on Scott's Web site.

Most clients meet with Scott at his office, where they see a size 60 Bears jersey, autographed by Perry, in a frame on the wall, and an autographed football in a display case.

And Gold/VIP Member Mike Miget gave Scott the idea of buying miniature Chicago Bears refrigerators, which were sold at The Home Depot, to give as gifts to the first ten people responding to mailings.

Scott cannot disclose the financial terms of his arrangements with "Refrigerator" Perry, but he assures me it would be affordable to many local small businesses.

---

### **Resource!**

---

Gold/VIP Member Dr. Barry Lycka used both national and local celebrities for marketing the grand opening of the Corona Rejuvenation Center and Spa. Susan Seaforth Hayes and Bill Hayes, stars of the NBC-TV soap opera "Days Of Our Lives," and Lynda Steele, the anchor of the TV news in the local market, all attended the grand opening and participated in its promotion. The sales letter Dr. Lycka sent to his patients and "VIP prospects" promoting this grand opening is provided at the end of this chapter (Exhibit #7, on pages 66–70). It's an outstanding example of using national and local celebrities, timing, drawings, gifts, and special offers all in one promotion.

Incidentally, well over 500 people attended this event!

Keep in mind that there are different ways to be a celebrity. A person can be instantly recognizable because of his or her face, such as a famous TV personality. Or a person might go unrecognized in a crowd but still have celebrity value based on who they are and what they do. Ford Motor Company was able to use former auto racing champion Jackie Stewart very effectively, even though you'd probably bump into him on the street and not know him. Even people who are not instantly recognizable visually or by name can still lend celebrity value and credibility to a marketing message once it is explained who they are.

How many of these names are instantly recognizable to you: Joan Quigley, Brendan Suhr, Robert Parker, and Linda Bloodworth-Thomason? If you got even one of them, you're sharper than most. Still, after telling you who they are, I can use each of them effectively in certain marketing messages.

Joan Quigley was Nancy Reagan's astrologer. I worked on an infomercial featuring Joan promoting books and cassettes about astrology. Brendan Suhr has been the assistant head coach of the Detroit Pistons and the Orlando Magic and could be used in marketing sports equipment, athletic shoes, or even, as I've used him, in promoting a self-improvement course. Robert Parker is the author of the famous "Spenser" detective novels, on which the TV series that starred Robert Urich was based. Parker would be an excellent personality to build a solve-a-mystery cruise package around. Linda Bloodworth-Thomason is a very successful TV producer; her credits include producing the hit show *Designing Women*. Linda could be used in marketing some kind of how-to-break-into-show-business product or a career success product for women.

In the production of TV infomercials I've worked with Florence Henderson, famous as the mom of *The Brady Bunch*; Gloria Loring, a soap opera actress; Robb Weller, former host of *Entertainment Tonight*; Robert Wagner, from *Hart to Hart* and the Austin Powers movies; and others. In marketing local projects, I've worked with local radio and television personalities in several cities. With only a few notable exceptions not named here, I've found both the celebrities and their agents to be pretty cooperative and pleasant to work with. Each of the ones I've named especially impressed me with his or her professionalism, ability, and sincere commitment to producing an effective project.

If you are seeking the services of a local celebrity, you can usually contact the person directly, or your advertising agency can track down the person for you and make a proposal. Many national celebrities can be found listed in the directories of the Academy of Motion Picture Arts and Sciences (available from Academy of Motion Pictures Arts and Sciences, 8949 Wilshire Boulevard, Beverly Hills, CA 90211, 310-247-3000). A free report on "How to Hire and Use Celebrities in Your Marketing" is available at *www.UltimateMarketingPlan.com*.

If you would like to see a great example of a local business using a local celebrity (a former local TV anchorman) very effectively in a successful ad, enroll in the free 12-Week Ultimate Marketing Plan Course delivered by e-mail, and watch for the newspaper page headlined EXPOSED: TV ANCHOR/REPORTER SPEAKS OUT AND REVEALS THE RAW TRUTH ABOUT THAT 'WORLD CLASS' MENSWEAR STORE THAT ADVERTISES IN THIS NEWSPAPER ALL THE TIME. You can enroll in the free course at *www.UltimateMarketingPlan.com.*

## The Impact of Bulk

I have a friend and colleague in the speaking business who has no brochure, no demo cassette, no professional selling tools at all. When someone is interested in booking him, my friend sends a box—the kind and size that holds 500 sheets of paper, like one you might buy at the office supply store—filled with copies of testimonial letters from his satisfied clients. I'm sure nobody sits and reads more than 400 letters. They don't have to.

Later in this chapter is a "client list" from a catering company (Exhibit #8, on pages 71–72). It, too, is impressive due to quantity.

## Testimonials Can Conquer the Toughest Marketing Challenges

Platinum Inner Circle Member Jerry Jones has to sell himself as a practice-building expert to dentists without being a dentist himself! Ten years ago, he bought a struggling, near-bankrupt marketing company he was working for, producing patient newsletters for dentists. He says he lay awake nights wondering what negative impact "not being one of them" would have. He marshaled a massive, impressive collection of testimonials from dentists who profited from the company's services and, as he puts it, "let these dentists do my talking for me." In all situations you are better served letting your customers do your talking for you, but that's doubly true in tough, difficult selling situations.

_____ **Resource!** _____

Get more information about Jerry Jones and his company's magazine, *Healthy, Wealthy & Wise*, by e-mailing him directly at *info@jerryjonesdirect.com*.

_____

Today, Jerry's company publishes a monthly magazine, *Healthy, Wealthy & Wise*, of which hundreds of thousands of copies are mailed each month to the patients of dentists, chiropractors, and MDs, and to financial advisors' clients. His company also provides turn-key direct-mail campaigns to dentists. And Jerry is even a highly paid marketing advisor to dentists, each paying him upward from $15,000.00 annually. All a testament to the power of testimonials!

Here's another tough case. Gold/VIP Member Darin Garman promotes the idea of investing in "heartland of America" apartment buildings and commercial properties. He sells Iowa properties to investors from all over the country. His first task is to convince them to enroll in his VIP Buyer's Program for a fee, long-distance, without ever meeting him or even talking with him! His second task is to convince them to invest hundreds of thousands of dollars in properties they've never seen, in a distant location. He accomplishes this with a masterfully written, very successful thirteen-page sales letter. I'd like you to see this entire example, so I've included it in its entirety in the 12-Week Ultimate Marketing Plan Course, delivered by e-mail, which you can get free at *www.UltimateMarketingPlan.com*.

And I have one more for you: My client and friend Tracy Tolleson provides a unique marketing system called The Pinnacle Club to mortgage brokers, one per area. The system enables the mortgage broker to "lock in" as many top Realtors as he likes, referring all of their loan business. The opportunity to use this system requires a fee of $19,000.00 to $29,000.00. To decide whether to join the program, the mortgage broker pays a deposit and travels to Phoenix to attend a meeting. At the end of the first day, the broker either decides "no," is refunded his deposit and leaves, or decides "yes" and pays the fee balance, signs contracts, and stays for training the second day. Keep in mind that the mortgage broker knows *in advance* that he's facing a price tag of $19,000.00 to $29,000.00! This, too, is accomplished with a powerful sales letter filled with factual, statistical, illustrated, and photographic proof. You can also see a copy of this letter in the 12-Week Ultimate Marketing Plan Course. If you are a mortgage professional with specific interest, request a copy of the letter and other information from Tolleson Mortgage Publications by faxing 602-269-3113.

## Use All the Fire Power You Can Muster

Today's smart marketer uses pictorial evidence, testimonials, client lists, satisfied customers, and celebrities—every ounce of social proof he can pull together—to prove his case.

### Resource!

A number of other outstanding sales letters featuring "preponderance of proof" and exceptionally effective use of testimonials are referenced in this book's companion, *The Ultimate Sales Letter*, and its linked 12-Week Course, at *www.Ultimate-Sales-Letter.com*.

**Exhibit #7**

January 3, 2005
Monday 7:32 a.m.

# Please Take Good Care of This Letter (and the attached key)

Dear Bill

Here's why you'll need to take good care of this letter (and the attached key). You'll need it to take advantage of the biggest preferred client event in Corona Rejuvenation Centre's history, to celebrate the grand opening of our new facility – when we become Corona Rejuvenation Centre and Spa. And this is your special invitation to attend.

You - and a very select group of our friends - get to take advantage of a special party "as a sneak peak" of our brand new 4200+ square foot facility, on February 14th (Valentine's day – the day of love- isn't that appropriate?).

Which brings us to the key. You need it to try and open

Here's how it works. Bring the key in this envelope and this letter and you can attempt to open our treasure box. The lucky person and a guest with the winning key will be will be jetted to beautiful Las Vegas on one of four weekends. You will be picked up in a limo and taken limo to

# The Bellagio

Las Vegas' five star hotel, and stay in a deluxe room overlooking their magnificent lake, where you can watch their amazing water and light show. Your hotel bill will be covered for four days and three nights. And you will have $500 USD for spending.

## **Exhibit #7** (continued)

But if you don't win the big prize, you will still be a winner. Your name will be entered into a draw for one of four genuine leather luggage sets.

And your name will be entered into a drawing for a one week vacation at a Worldmark resort. Valid at 70 resorts in The coastal U.S., Hawaii, Australia, Fiji and Canada – you can go just about anywhere.

*WorldMark*
Trendwest

Plus everyone in attendance will receive a free gift.
When you arrive, we have this special gift waiting for you - A compact with a calculator. These are specially made for this event and are sure to be collectors items (but come early -- there are only enough for the first 297 people).

And you will receive a certificate for a free AFA Clay Peel™ designed to remove fine lines, rough skin, and pigment irregularities. And everyone will receive certificates for a complimentary cosmetic analysis and 10% off any procedure we sell.

But there's more... Corona will be introducing a

## NEW SECRET FRAGRANCE

Scientifically designed, Corona's New Aroma, is an essential oil developed exclusively for our spa. Contrary to rumor, it **does not contain sexual attractants.** But, oh, what this does for you and those around you.

## Take An Extra 10% Off Everything You Buy Today
## (including gift certificates)
## (Isn't that convenient with Valentine's Day coming the next day?)

**Exhibit #7** (continued)

Never have so many money-saving opportunities been combined into one event. You can buy all services and products at 10% our regular prices ((please don't tell my accountant). And we will give an extra 10% to the Lurana shelter, an organization that provides temporary shelter for women with or without children who are victims of domestic violence. This will be ear marked for their resource center, which desperately needs resources.

# It Starts Sunday, February 14
# From 4 - 8 p.m.

We're going to have this special event on Sunday, February 13th - the day before the day of love – because you are such a special person and we know how much Corona Rejuvenation Centre's new facility will mean to you.

You see, what thrills us the most is helping you and so many others like you achieve the looks you want. And if you look good, you feel good, and vice versa. These are exciting times in that there is so much to offer you to improve your skin, the way you feel, and the way you want to look.

### Not An Ordinary Party

And believe me, this won't be just an ordinary, run of the mill kind of party. First, there will be a festive and a festive atmosphere where we can all relax and you can learn more about what we do here.

Second, we have arranged some special guests.

Susan Seaforth Hayes and Doug Hayes of Days of Our Lives will be on hand. You know them as Doug and Julie Williams and they will be here meet and greet you. Don't forget your camera!!!!!!

And Lynda Steele, co-anchor of Global Television's 6 and 11 o'clock news will also be on hand to meet you.

**Exhibit #7** (continued)

# Great Food and Drink

There will be great food and drink from caterers, and white gloved severs to make this a special event

## Learn about the special things we have to offer .......

Corona will have special demo's and information on the following:

*How you can get rid of unwanted hair with IPL and Laser our laser hair services*
Corona was the first centre in Edmonton to offer laser hair removal services and we are into out 7th generation of machines. These are faster, more predictable, more comfortable than ever. We are the only center in Edmonton that **GUARANTEES** permanent hair reduction.

*How to lift and tighten your skin nonsurgically with Thermage (as seen on Oprah)*
The non-surgical facelift / browlift technology uses a unique form of radio frequency energy to produce a desired cosmetic or therapeutic effect without damaging skin. ThermaLift can safely improve the appearance of skin in various areas including the eye area (crow's feet), lower face (jowls), forehead and neck. ThermaLift is also approved in the treatment of acne and acne scarring.

*Learn about the wonders of massage (and sign up for one with your significant other  the same time)*
Do you feel stressed? Need to relax? Have muscle aches and pains? Suffer from back problems? Sports injuries? Need body toning. Then our massage is for you.

*See our extensive line of wonderful products* – tailor made just for you

*See how we can turn back the clock on your skin with Photo Rejuvenation for the aging face and hands* with our Quantun and Starlux IPL's – the most advanced in the business.

*Find out more about Glo minerals.* Does your make-up glow? Glo mineral make-up offers a revolutionary good for you make-up that delivers a flawless face. Oil-free, light reflecting, synthetic/fragrance free, SPF 15 make-up line perfect for all skin types. *"Flawless skin is everyone's dream. Glo Minerals make it a reality."*

# Exhibit #7 (concluded)

*Reshape your body, lose weight, get rid of cellulite, cellulite and stress relief with Endermologie™, Mesotherapy, and Lipodissolve-* Now you can get rid of unwanted fat and cellulite without needles, without pain with our new technology

*Look great with a fantasy tan without tanning with Fantasy tan*

*Enjoy a pedicure, manicure, facial or microdermabrasion*

*Lift falling buttocks, faces and breast with the new acthyderm system.*

*Sign up for a free AFA clay peel. cosmetic analysis and Glo® makeover.*

This invitation is for you and only you! I expect a large turnout – so in order that you are certain to get in you must call and register 425-885. Space is limited and many have already called and secured their place, **so call now!**

I look forward so much to seeing you at our Grand Opening day – no work, just fun and plenty of information.

Oh - **don't forget** - you will also have the opportunity to book any procedure at a significant discount at this event, only on this day, an amazing opportunity too good to pass up!

Leah Walsh

PS: OK, I relent – you can bring a friend, but just one– but please call! Remember this event is for 4 hours on February 13, 2004. . Plus the key in this letter entitles you to a chance to win A FREE 4 DAY/3 NIGHT VACATION in Las Vegas.

*10% discount requires payment in full by cash, check, or credit card.

Here's a picture of your free gift – an extremely attractive and practical compact style calculator! Sure to be the handiest item in your purse! Yours just for coming in! Plus a free clay peel and a certificate for a free cosmetic analysis.

And don't forget to come and meet the stars – Season Seaforth and Doug Hayes and Lynda Steele.

P.P.S. We always like to help others –and this event will also be used for this. 10% of all purchases will be used to support the Lurana shelter to help with our commitment to help abused women.

# Exhibit #8

## Sharko's

4522 N. 26th Drive • Phoenix, Arizona 85017 • (602) 242-2662

### Catering For All Occasions
*...Good Food...Good Service...*

SHARKO'S CATERING has been serving the entire valley for over thirteen years. We look forward to be of service to you for any occasion.

We are proud to announce some of our previous clients:

Catered to POPE JOHN PAUL II ENTOURAGE while in Phoenix

| | |
|---|---|
| Weddings | |
| Cookouts | |
| Open Houses | |
| Anniversaries | |
| Church Functions | |
| Office Parties | |

Lou Grubb Car Dealership
Knoell Homes
Citibank
Century 21
The Hartford Insurance
Sears Stores
The Salvation Army
IBM
U.S.Express
Bradshaw & Viles
Serra Club
Kino Institute
Frazee Paint
United Pacific Insurance
Grunewald & Adams Fine Jewelers
Gannett Outdoor Co.
Skyway Management
MeraBank
Del E. Webb Corp.
U.S. West Directory
Arizona Lift Trucks
C.G. Rein Galleries
Sun Cities Art Museum
Nike
Heidelberg West

The Catholic Diocese of Phoenix
U.S. Navy Reserves
U.S. Marine Reserves
Society for Neuroscience
The Greyhound Corp.
Penneys Stores
Boys Club of Phoenis
Mardian Construction
Climate Control
MCI
Carson Messinger Elliot, etc.
   (law firm)
Crampton Woods etc.(law firm)
O'Connor, Cavanaugh (law firm)
Air National Guard of Arizona
Simplex Time Recorder Co.
Blood Systems, Inc.
Desert X--Rays
Arizona Special Olympics
M/V Acceptance, Ltd.
Scottsdale Resort Apt. Hotel
Temple Solel
Cigna
The Arizona Republic/Phoenix Gazette

## SHARKO'S CLIENT LIST, P. 1

## Exhibit #8 (concluded)

### Sharko's

4522 N 26th Drive • Phoenix, Arizona 85017 • (602) 242-2662
Catering For All Occasions
*...Good Food...Good Service...*

Weddings

– 2 –

Cookouts

Open Houses

Anniversaries

Church Functions

Office Parties

Levitz Furniture Corp.
U.S. Recycling
DMJM
Eason & Waller
Phoenix Heat Treating Corp.
Phoenix Distr. Co.
Phillips & Lyon (law firm)
Amica Insurance
Transamerica Insurance
Systems Marketing, Inc.
Neutron Industries
Realty Executives
Continental Insurance
Casa Santa Cruz
American Resort Residential
      Developers, Inc.
Dun &Bradstreet
Dial One
Telemation
Goldwater Stores
Murray Peck, P.C.
Fremont Indemnity Co.
Mazak
Hill Bros. Chemical Co.
Linda Brock car dealership
Lynndale Stainless Service, Inc.
Rivera & Scales, P.C.
Lyon Commercial Brokerage Co.
Nevada Federal Credit Union
National Brands, Inc.

Sun Insurance Agency
The Sun Eagle Corp.
P A C of Arizona
Powerwall Corp.
Presto Casting Co.
Phoenix & Valley of the Sun
      Convention & Visitors Bureau
Prestige Cleaners
Realty World
Eastman Kodak Co.
Scientific-Atlanta
Sun City Water Co.
P.I.P.E.
Swiss-America Trading Corp.
Western International University
Turf Paradise, Inc.
Select Drywall
Shannon & Cronin  (law firm)
Valley National Bank
Tech Plastics Inc.
Turner Ranches
Valley Neurology Associates, Ltd.
Harris Data Service
Wisniewski Surrano (law firm)
Westernaires
The  Tanner Companies
Westbrook Village
DeMuro Enterprises, Inc.
American Home Shield
Louis P. Ferrara (law firm)
+ many, many more!

## SHARKO'S CLIENT LIST, P. 2

# Putting Your Best Foot Forward

I have, on many occasions, been paid as a consultant to visit a chiropractor's office, tour it, check out the office's new-patient procedures, and evaluate what might be done better in order to make patients comfortable, confident, satisfied, and likely to refer. Frankly, an amazing number of times, my best advice has had to do with some 75-watt light bulbs and a bottle of Mr. Clean. Which brings us to a discussion of image; specifically, "business image."

Let's begin inside your business, at its premises. This is relevant to the degree that your customers, vendors, investors, or community members visit your business location. If no one ever visits, there's nominal damage done by a pigsty location. If even one person visits, the damage begins.

The Minit-Lube example is instructive; these guys stole an entire business right out from under the service-station owners and operators, virtually overnight, with a remarkably simple strategy: a pleasant environment. Perhaps you've taken your car to a service station and waited while getting an oil change. The waiting area had old, peeling linoleum covered with grease and two plastic chairs to sit on; a stack of hot-rod magazines; and a coffeemaker surrounded by Styrofoam cups and utensils. Now, with that memory clearly fixed in your mind, go visit a Minit-Lube (or any of its regional kindred, such as Jiffy Lube). I don't need to describe the difference. Or the difference it has made in where America gets its oil changed.

Another industry that has undergone a similar metamorphosis is the instant, or storefront, printing business. That business has been reinvented by Kinkos.

These innovators have applied lessons learned from Walt Disney and Ray Kroc: even simple cleanliness can be a powerful marketing tool.

Here's a very simple, two-question test to apply to your own business premises and everything that is seen, heard, touched, smelled, tasted, or experienced there:

### Question #1
In ten words or less, describe the image you want your business to project.

### Question #2
Does *everything* contribute to projecting that image?

Let me give you a great example of incongruity. For most of my life, I've owned and driven Ford and Lincoln-Mercury vehicles. Currently I have a big, fat, gas-guzzling SUV and I'm proud of it. But one time, I had a Cadillac. When I had my Caddy, I had it serviced at the best, most successful, most respected Cadillac dealership in Phoenix. As you might guess, its new-car showroom was immaculate: windows sparkling clean, floor buffed to a high gloss, lighting just so, unobtrusive music playing softly in the background.

Their service department was also smartly run. During morning rush hour, when many people dropped off their cars, neatly dressed young women greeted the customers and offered them coffee. The service technicians also were nicely dressed, with shirts and neckties. The area was kept pretty much free of grease and grime. There was also an air of efficiency that was reassuring. The service technicians each had a computer terminal and could pull up your car's service records. From the screen, they knew and didn't have to ask for your name, address, phone number, etc.

So far, so good.

The first incongruity was, I suppose, relatively minor, yet it certainly made a major, lasting impression on my mind: the courtesy cars they used to drop customers off at their offices were Buicks, not Cadillacs.

The second incongruity looms larger: the place where you settled your account was sandwiched into a narrow hallway; you stood not in a line, for which there was no room, but rather in an intimate, pushing, annoying cluster of people; you conversed with the clerks through tiny little windows; and the clerk I dealt with on two occasions chewed and popped bubblegum and was devoid of personality.

What's wrong with that picture? A lot. To be consistent with the image being conveyed by all other areas of the operation, there should have been a nicely appointed, living-room type of area where the customers sat comfortably and the clerks came to them, got the invoices signed, took the credit cards back to the accounting area, processed them there, and brought the finished paperwork back to the customer with a smile and a thank-you.

## ULTIMATE MARKETING SECRET WEAPON #8
### Image Congruency

Every piece of your "puzzle" should be strategically crafted to reinforce a single, central image.

I'd suggest, incidentally, that "successful" be part of the image you choose to convey. I find that, in most businesses, customers prefer dealing with successful businesses and successful businesspeople.

I can recall going with a consulting client of mine when he was interviewing and choosing a new attorney for his firm. His company was in considerable difficulty with the Federal Trade Commission at the time, so he was going to be a fat catch for whichever law firm he selected. I thought the conversation with the two lawyers at the first firm went well, but he was skeptical about them when we left. He admitted that he couldn't put his finger on why he was uncomfortable with them; he just was. It was several hours later that the impression maneuvered from his subconscious to his conscious and he was able to enunciate his reason for discomfort: "Nothing," he said, "was going on." The phones weren't ringing; the receptionist was reading a magazine; there were empty word-processor work areas; there was no typing noise. In his mind he translated that—rightly or wrongly, but in marketing, perception is reality—to mean that the law firm was unsuccessful.

Once I was counseling a chiropractor, brand-new in practice, located in a brand-new shopping center that was at a busy intersection but too new to be fully occupied with tenants. He was suffering from an inordinately high number of "no shows": people who would respond to his advertising, schedule exam appointments, and then not show up.

His parking lot was empty.

He and his staff parked their own cars behind the center. His practice was so new that there were rarely patients' cars parked in the lot, and there were no adjacent tenants creating traffic. "How would you feel," I asked him, "if you started to drive up here for your first appointment?"

We got his car, his staff's cars, and a couple of rented-by-the-week Cadillacs parked in front of that office; his no-show rate dropped like a rock.

## Creating a Marketing-Oriented Store Environment

If you don't have a store, you're welcome to skip this brief section.

Coincidentally and fortunately, I was at a major shopping mall recently, and, in a national chain store I won't name here, I overheard one well-dressed woman, apparently rather affluent, say to her shopping companion, "Let's go—this place is too confusing. I can't find what I want here."

I can't count how many times I've seen a store environment or at least part of a store environment designed for the convenience of the staff—not the customer! The smart store environment quite simply facilitates buying. That should be the primary consideration in every design and display decision: does it make it easier and more likely that the customer will buy?

Last week, I was in a men's clothing store and was struck by these oddities:

1. The casual slacks, like jeans and twill slacks, were intermingled with the dress slacks.
2. The necktie display was closer to the sport shirts than to the dress shirts.
3. Shoes were displayed only in the window, and then all the way at the rear of the store.
4. The walls in the dressing rooms were blank.

What would you do differently?

I think I'd group my sports clothes together in one area, and display casual slacks, shirts, jackets, and shoes there. I'd similarly group my dress slacks, dress shirts, ties, jackets, suits, and dress shoes together. I'd put framed photos of my newest fashions and framed testimonial letters up on the walls of the dressing rooms.

Here's my Five-Point Criteria for smart store design:

1. Conveys a congruent, deliberate image.
2. Presents goods in a logical, organized way.
3. Helps the customer think with "creative idea displays."

(I was in a pet store recently and—lo and behold—in the fish section, they had a display featuring everything you'd need to set up your first tropical fish aquarium: the aquarium itself, the underground filter, a bag of gravel, a stand, a light and hood, and so on, each neatly labeled with what it was and what it did. Over by the cute puppies was a similar display titled "The Family's First Dog," and it displayed a bowl, a bag of food, a box of vitamins, a couple of chew toys, a brush, a collar, a leash, and so on.)

4. Educates the customer when appropriate—by display, by continuous-loop video, by live demonstrator.
5. Utilizes every possibility—such as wall space—to promote, advertise, and educate.

_____ **Resource!** _____

The number one marketing advisor to retailers is Bill Glazer, and you can get free reports and information from him at *www.bgsmarketing. com*. More than 10,000 retailers in menswear, ladieswear, sporting goods, jewelry, and other categories use Bill's ads, mailings, in-store signage and display strategies, customer rewards programs, and other business development tools.

Some store environment principles apply to non-store locations, too, even including professional offices. I teach chiropractors, for example, that there are only three reasons for the patient being in the office:

1. To get well
2. To learn how to stay well
3. To get inspired to refer

Every minute that a patient spends there, and everything seen or heard while there, should be related to one, two, or all three of those reasons. That means: out with the magazines, in with interesting, educational literature; out with the background music, in with continuous-loop video; out with the mass-produced paintings of farmhouses and snowcapped mountains, in with charts and posters.

An accountant accidentally heard me talking to a group of chiropractors about this and cornered me after the seminar. "How can I apply that idea to my office?" he wanted to know. I asked him, "What are your clients there for? What services do you offer that most clients need but few use?"

We agreed that his clients were there, first, to get well organized financially; second, to learn how to work in tandem with him to stay that way; and third, to get inspired to refer. We determined that financial planning and estate planning were little-used services. So, out with the magazines, in with interesting, educational literature about financial planning and estate planning; out with the generic paintings, in with relevant posters and signs. And, without a nickel of external advertising, his practice increased its total services rendered to existing clients by more than 30 percent and doubled its client base through referrals in a year.

I think just about any business can turn its environment into a much more effective marketing-oriented environment with these ideas.

One of the finest examples amongst my clientele is Gold/VIP Member Dr. Charles Martin's cosmetic dentistry practice in Richmond, Virginia. His brand of "Smile Dentistry" is designed for people with complex or difficult dental situations, often involving complete makeovers. His target clientele is affluent individuals who value and can afford first-class care and will invest in comprehensive treatment programs.

He says that, in 2003, while I was in his office consulting with him, he had an epiphany: to attract, inspire trust in, and satisfy the type of patients he most desired, from the local population and from all across the country, he needed to create a unique physical environment that made an appropriate statement and provided far more than these patients would expect. The result was a complete office makeover, which I'll briefly describe here:

Dr. Martin's reception area now has an Italian marble terrazzo floor, café tables like those you'd find in front of a European café, high-speed Internet access stations, and another section with comfortable chairs and couches. Nestled away in a corner, there's a PlayStation gaming area. Patients feel like they are in an exclusive clubroom. Accompanying spouses or friends can relax with a cup of fresh-brewed cappuccino or latte, check their e-mail, even conduct business over the Internet while waiting. The reading material in the lounge features patient before/after scrapbooks, and books of testimonials. There is also a patient education theater, where people can view videos about Martin Method Dentistry. Oh, and did I mention the beautiful grand piano with the "secret" CD player, so that it plays itself? Walls are graced with original art but also with photographs of patients showing off their newly acquired perfect smiles, along with their written success stories.

Before, during, or after dental treatment, patients can also visit The Spa Room, with a heated massage chair, relaxing music, scented candles, even paraffin hand wax treatment. In the dental treatment rooms, the dental chairs have temperature-sensitive body-cuddling foam pads and massage pads. Headphones are provided, with music pre-selected by the patient. (For me, Sinatra.) Some patients sleep through their dental work, too.

On the way out, patients leave with their favorite kind of homemade, fresh-baked cookies. Yes—fresh-baked every morning there at the office, placed in bags closed with ribbons.

Patients are impressed. Patients can't resist telling their friends and associates about their amazing experience. And referred patients come from all over the country, flying over thousands of dentists, to get to Dr. Martin.

Dentists or other professionals reading this can get more information at *AffluentPracticeSystems.com.*

Does this seem extreme to you?

Is your instant knee-jerk reaction "not appropriate to my business"?

It's appropriate if you want extreme success!

## Boosting Your Image with Brand-Name Identity

For years, when you went to the grocery store or supermarket to buy some chicken for the Saturday afternoon backyard barbeque, you bought chicken, period. Just chicken, on a cardboard tray, wrapped with plastic wrap by the grocer. But Frank Perdue used himself as a spokesperson and his name to proprietize chicken, and today people go to the store looking for Perdue Chicken. Of course, there's also Jimmy Dean Sausage and Bob Evans Farm Sausage.

In some areas of the country, if you look in your Yellow Pages under "Plumbing," you may find a big ad featuring George Brazil Plumbing, with a choice of phone numbers for different areas in your locale. And if you call, the plumber who comes to your home will be in a clean, neatly pressed uniform with the George Brazil logo.

Actually, this is nothing more than an advertising identity, a form of a brand name, which individual plumbers in each area pay for the right to use. This gives each plumber a big image boost over other independent operators.

## How Do You Decide Which Movie to See?

I've always found the movie I wanted to see and then gone to whatever theater it was playing at that was closest to my house, and I'm sure others use that same process. But a recent "Best of Phoenix" survey showed me that a lot of moviegoers use a very different process: they prefer and deliberately choose to go to Harkins Theaters. Here in our area we have theaters owned by several national chains, such as General Theaters. Harkins happens to be a small, locally owned chain, and its brand name is recognized by many theatergoers as number one in quality and value. This chain has the cleanest theaters, most comfortable seats, and best gourmet snacks. Many people look in the newspaper first for Harkins' ads, then choose among the movies playing at Harkins, rather than choosing a movie first and then deciding on the theater. It proves that even a small, local business can create strong brand-name identity in the marketplace and profit tremendously as a result.

## A Warning about "Putting Your Best Foot Forward"

Since I wrote the first and second editions of this book, I think consumers have become more demanding about the "experience" they have when patronizing a store, restaurant, professional practice, or service provider. Gold and Gold+ Glazer-Kennedy Inner Circle Members get a special memo from me each month, on a different, timely marketing topic. Here's one from 2004 that I believe is especially relevant:

◆ ◆ ◆

### *Even Being Great Is No Longer Good Enough*

Tom Peters' most recent book, *Re-imagine*, is a provocative book. Here are a few pickings from the book, with my comments.

> "If we use terms such as 'experience,' we limit them to Starbucks or Disney. Instead we must apply them to the IBM's. . . ."

It IS no longer enough to think in terms of or to deliver "excellence" in your core goods or services or quality or service. We now live in, to borrow another book's title, an EXPERIENCE ECONOMY, where the consumer must be given some kind of meaningful, interesting, entertaining, involving, and memorable experience. And Tom's right: when we talk about this, we too often invoke the same few, obvious demonstrations, like Disney and Starbucks, when the challenge, the mandate is to apply it to every kind of business. To YOUR business.

"Harley-Davidson does not sell motorcycles. Starbucks does not sell coffee. Guinness does not sell beer. Think about it."

A Harley exec said: "What we sell is the ability/opportunity/excuse for a forty-three-year-old accountant to dress in black leather, ride through small towns and have people fear them—the Rebel Experience." A visit to a Restoration Hardware store is a nostalgia experience.

A business, like a novel, should have a plot.

---

## Resource!

I recommend reading Tom Peters's book, *Re-imagine*, and Howard Schultz's book about Starbucks, *Pour Your Heart Into It*, for more ideas about creating extraordinary customer experiences. Also, you can get a free 3-month trial Gold Inner Circle Membership at *www.UltimateMarketingPlan.com*.

---

Peters uses different catalogs, some with novel-like plots, others missing it. As a writer, I think it's a very good point. This is yet another way to think about, to get at, a USP. A point of view. Think about popular TV shows, past and present. Most have the same basic recurring plot, known to its fans. *CSI*: murder under unusual and mystifying circumstances, defiant killer, scientific deduction. *The A-Team*: somebody, usually damsel, in distress. Outmatched, out-gunned heroes outwit villains, save damsel. *I Love Lucy*: Lucy gets into trouble, trying to do good. She and Ethel attempt to conceal the mess from Ricky and Fred, at which point it gets worse. Hijinks ensue.

What's your business's plot? What do your customers/clients/patients share with you, as a fundamental understanding of who you are, what you're about, what to look forward to? For a few years now, Bill Glazer's retail stores' plot has been exciting offers featuring a different, interesting premium/free gift each time. His yearly off-premises, at-the-fairgrounds sale had a plot; two years ago, he kept the sale, changed the plot. Gold+ Glazer-Kennedy Inner Circle Member Dr. Gregg Nielsen's practice operates currently with two plots. One is the *I Love Lucy* plot: his employees have gotten into trouble; they are trying to cover it up or fix it and get out of the doghouse; hijinks ensue. (You can see a Dr. Nielsen campaign in the free 12-Week Ultimate Marketing Plan Course. Sign up at *www.UltimateMarketingPlan.com*.)

Here are some idea-starters:

## Was vs. Is . . .

| WAS | IS |
| --- | --- |
| Product/Service | Experience |
| Quality | A kick, a hoot |
| It works | Leaves an indelible memory |
| Satisfied customer | Member of a club |
| Meets needs | Defines who you are |

## Common vs. Different

| COMMON | DIFFERENT |
| --- | --- |
| Coffee | Starbucks |
| Underwear | Victoria's Secret |
| Atlantic City | Atlantis, Paradise Island |
| CNN | Fox News |

# Getting Free Advertising

I'll bet you've heard the old adage, "There's no such thing as bad press." It is often quoted. It's also ridiculous. Ask some of the companies that have been destroyed, and I do mean destroyed, some justly but some unjustly, by TV news programs such as *20/20* or *60 Minutes*. Yes, you can tell it's going to be a bad day when Mike Wallace is waiting for you when you arrive at the office.

The first rule of getting good publicity is to avoid bad publicity.

## Publicity and Public Relations

Some years back, in an incredibly stupid move, America West Airlines published an article in its company newsletter by one of its preferred-provider doctors in which he called the chiropractic profession "a cult" and compared chiropractic treatment to "a shampoo and a set."

The MD who wrote this article must have been on another planet when the chiropractic profession had previously won its lawsuit against the AMA, prompted by just such remarks as that one. But it is inconceivable that a large, generally smartly run corporation would permit material certain to be offensive to a large constituency to appear in print under its name.

The backlash was fast and big. *The Chiropractic Journal*, a newspaper with a reach that includes about 10,000 chiropractors in America West's prime market areas of Arizona, Nevada, and California, devoted not just column inches but pages to savaging the airline. Hundreds of chiropractors called and canceled flight reservations. Practice-management firms holding meetings urged attending practitioners to fly other airlines. Many Phoenix chiropractors distributed literature criticizing the airline to all of their patients.

I can't speculate about what the airline lost as a result of all this. It could have been worse; the airline was fortunate that the local news media didn't make a story out of it. But I can tell you that they won nothing and lost something. The person at the helm of a business has to carefully scrutinize every advertisement, press release, publication, verbal statement, product name—everything—and ask one question: Is there any way this can blow up in my face?

In the entertainment business, there's a country-and-western singer who did immeasurable damage to her career by attacking the beef industry. She may have thought the media attention of the moment was pretty nifty, but over the long haul she's found sponsors for concerts and TV shows, guest invitations to talk shows, and other important advantages hard to come by. Of course, more recently, Oprah made some negative comments about that same industry, was sued but prevailed, and apparently has not suffered at all. However, Oprah is Oprah.

Some years ago, the media and the public went into such a blood frenzy when Donald Trump's marital and financial troubles surfaced that the negative publicity scared his bankers half to death and nearly toppled his entire empire. He came within a hair's breadth of destruction, thanks to bad PR.

As I'm writing this, another edition of Trump's *The Apprentice* TV show has just ended, and The Donald is so hot he's on fire. He has astutely and aggressively capitalized on the media spotlight turned on by *The Apprentice* to quickly pump out two bestselling books and secure endorsement deals from VISA, a fragrance company, a clothing company, and even a hair-care products company! Even current bad PR about his financially troubled casinos has barely been a blip against the much bigger positive PR that he's worked hard to create. I spoke at an event late in 2004, where I immediately followed Donald Trump, and I can tell you from firsthand experience, people love this guy. At the moment, the outrageous Mr. Trump is riding high!

Sometimes being "outrageous" works, sometimes not. But when you are offensive and get your publicity by offending people, you may find the backlash more destructive than the original attention was helpful. There are less radical and risky approaches.

## Resource!

In recognition of the public's fascination with *The Apprentice*, we booked first-year winner Bill Rancic to speak at the Glazer-Kennedy Inner Circle 2005 Marketing & Moneymaking SuperConference, and my Platinum Member and client Rory Fatt booked first-year competitor Kristi Frank, part owner of a restaurant, to speak at his Restaurant Marketing Boot Camp. Information about all of our events can be accessed through *www.UltimateMarketingPlan.com*. A free report about using celebrities in your advertising and marketing is at that same Web site.

# How to Get Favorable Media Attention and Publicity: Joining Forces with a Charity

For a number of years, a business associate of mine did a fantastic job of aligning his stores with the Phoenix Chapter of the Arthritis Foundation. By very actively supporting its annual telethon with fundraising activities, personnel, and his personal assistance, he was able to obtain a large amount of free, positive publicity on radio and television. And the contacts he made in the media through this activity proved of continuous and frequent value in promoting his business in other ways.

On a bigger, national level, Bill Phillips, former CEO of the sports nutrition company EAS, got massive, favorable media attention for his book *Body For Life* by donating proceeds to the Make-A-Wish Foundation. Many companies have linked their businesses to former Secretary of State Colin Powell's nonprofit organization, America's Promise, which provides resources to at-risk kids. A national eyeglass chain, for example, donated hundreds of thousands of pairs of glasses and free eye exams. Amongst other things, this got that company mentioned by Colin Powell in just about every speech he gave for several years—though there's no way they could have hired him as a celebrity spokesperson.

Most charities and nonprofit organizations welcome the interest of any business owner who might assist them in their fundraising activities. You'll probably be surprised at how easy it is to get involved and how little it takes in fundraising capability to be considered a VIP by the organization, especially on a local level.

Just as one example, I have a client, Rod Smith, a former NFL star, who puts on nearly a hundred football-and-character-building youth camps in cities and towns all across America every summer. On a local level, a company can be a major sponsor for as little as a few thousand dollars. That gets the company plenty of name recognition, publicity, literature distributed to the kids and their parents, and the added value of doing something genuinely useful in the community. (Rod's company, Dynamic Sports, is in Scottsdale, Arizona.)

So, what can you do? Using special promotions and collection displays such as coin cans in your place of business, you can raise money for the charity from your customers. Take a lesson from national companies such as 7–11 and Dairy Queen and the countless others that donate a penny, nickel, or dime for every so many items sold during a promotional period. With the charity's permission, you can use this in your advertising and as a letter to seek free advertising.

You can also raise funds for the charity through your own employees and their friends and relatives. Activities such as bowl-a-thons, walk-a-thons, and 10K races give your employees an opportunity to get pledges of $x$ cents per pin or per mile from their friends, and then an opportunity to participate and have fun. Even a small group of ten employees who each get ten people to pledge fifty cents a pin for a bowl-a-thon can collectively raise hundreds of dollars, even a thousand dollars or more.

By running several customer/public promotions and several employee activities during the half-year prior to the charity's telethon or other major fundraising event, your business can come to the party with a donation of $5,000.00, $10,000.00, or more, and be viewed as a major contributor—and all without actually taking bottom-line dollars to make a contribution. If you match that with some dollars diverted from your ad budget, you can be a major player.

A word to the wise: choose your charity carefully. A group formed to preserve historic buildings in your community might sound good until it gets into conflict with the city government's plans to plop a new industrial park on that same site, bringing 2,000 new jobs to town. A feed-the-homeless program may sound great until a few of the homeless people frequenting the soup kitchen make news by burglarizing nearby homes and parked cars.

Local chapters of recognized, reputable national organizations such as the Arthritis, Leukemia, or Easter Seals foundations are usually safe and do provide a useful collection of benefits to their respective constituencies.

For your self-interest, you'll want to choose an organization that is highly visible in your community and very aggressive and progressive in its promotional activities. Frankly, there's no point in clutching the coattails of someone who's not going anywhere. An organization that has a locally *televised* telethon, auction, rodeo, or other major activity is ideal.

For the benefit of others, I encourage you to choose an organization with a policy of low overhead and high pass-through of funds in ways that genuinely help ill, handicapped, or disadvantaged people. There are unfortunately a number of nonprofits that use up most of their money on bureaucratic overhead, salaries, and fundraising rather than doing anything with it that genuinely helps people. You should also try to find an activity or organization you honestly feel is making an important contribution to society, so you get some psychic reward from your support and can create employee morale and customer loyalty with sincere enthusiasm for the cause you all join in supporting. (Personally, I've long been a supporter of Habitat for Humanity, which builds housing for the poor but insists that the recipients contribute "sweat equity.")

One of our Gold+ Glazer-Kennedy Inner Circle Members, a student and user of my marketing for more than twenty years—who frequently does a terrific job with charity tie-ins—is small-town chiropractor Dr. Gregg Nielsen. Shown here in Exhibit #9 are two simple sales letters Dr. Nielsen used one October and November, mailed to past, "lost" patients, current patients, and others who had expressed interest in his services. Each letter includes a brief mention of a donation to the community's fire department. Also shown, the photograph and caption that appeared in the local newspaper—free advertising! This promotion brought 110 patients in the door, from a very small mailing.

Another great example comes from Bill Glazer, linking his stores' Fiftieth Anniversary promotions to Habitat for Humanity via a celebrity-autographed-tie auction. This is such an ingenious example, because it incorporates use of both celebrity and charity tie-in (Exhibit #10).

Dr. Barry Lycka, a business and marketing consultant to cosmetic surgeons, frequently relies on publicity to promote his own practice. He received coverage in more than 100 newspapers nationwide when he initiated a program providing free cosmetic surgery to victims of domestic abuse.

## Exhibit #9

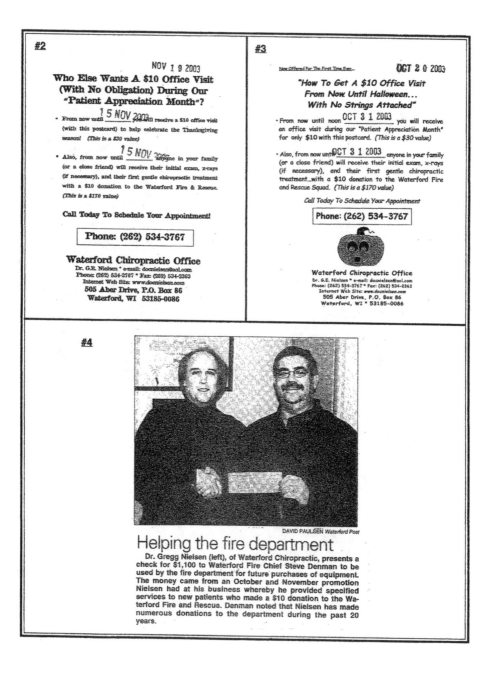

**#2**

NOV 1 9 2003

**Who Else Wants A $10 Office Visit (With No Obligation) During Our "Patient Appreciation Month"?**

- From now until 1 5 NOV 2003 will receive a $10 office visit (with this postcard) to help celebrate the Thanksgiving season! *(This is a $30 value)*

- Also, from now until 1 5 NOV 2003 anyone in your family (or a close friend) will receive their initial exam, x-rays (if necessary), and their first gentle chiropractic treatment with a $10 donation to the Waterford Fire & Rescue. *(This is a $170 value)*

**Call Today To Schedule Your Appointment!**

**Phone: (262) 534-3767**

**Waterford Chiropractic Office**
Dr. G.E. Nielsen * e-mail: docnielsen@aol.com
Phone: (262) 534-3767 * Fax: (262) 534-2363
Internet Web Site: www.docnielsen.com
505 Aber Drive, P.O. Box 86
Waterford, WI 53185-0086

**#3**

Now Offered For The First Time Ever...  OCT 2 0 2003

**"How To Get A $10 Office Visit From Now Until Halloween... With No Strings Attached"**

- From now until noon OCT 3 1 2003 you will receive an office visit during our "Patient Appreciation Month" for only $10 with this postcard. *(This is a $30 value)*

- Also, from now until OCT 3 1 2003 anyone in your family (or a close friend) will receive their initial exam, x-rays (if necessary), and their first gentle chiropractic treatment...with a $10 donation to the Waterford Fire and Rescue Squad. *(This is a $170 value)*

*Call Today To Schedule Your Appointment*

**Phone: (262) 534-3767**

**Waterford Chiropractic Office**
Dr. G.E. Nielsen * e-mail: docnielsen@aol.com
Phone: (262) 534-3767 * Fax: (262) 534-2363
Internet Web Site: www.docnielsen.com
505 Aber Drive, P.O. Box 86
Waterford, WI * 53185-0086

**#4**

DAVID PAULSEN *Waterford Post*

## Helping the fire department

Dr. Gregg Nielsen (left), of Waterford Chiropractic, presents a check for $1,100 to Waterford Fire Chief Steve Denman to be used by the fire department for future purchases of equipment. The money came from an October and November promotion Nielsen had at his business whereby he provided specified services to new patients who made a $10 donation to the Waterford Fire and Rescue. Denman noted that Nielsen has made numerous donations to the department during the past 20 years.

## Exhibit #10

*Gage World Class Mens Store*

# Signatures on Silk

Since 1946, Gage World Class Mens Stores has been a part of the Baltimore community. In celebration of our 50th Anniversary and our desire to thank Baltimore for its support, Gage is hosting a celebrity tie silent auction to benefit Chesapeake Habitat for Humanity. The auction will consist of framed, autographed neckties from local, national, and international celebrities.

The autographed ties will be on display one week at each store, allowing all our customers an opportunity to see and bid on their favorite celebrity. There will be over 50 autographed ties displayed, including:

| | | | | | |
|---|---|---|---|---|---|
| •Bob Dole | •Brooks Robinson | •Clyde Drexler | •Linda Sherman | •Jerry Springer | •Don Johnson |
| •Nolan Ryan | •Jim Palmer | •Rod Laver | •Tom Davis | •Bob Hope | •Gerald McRaney |
| •Buzz Aldrin | •Eddie Murray | •Mike Schmidt | •Mike Thomas | •Alex Trebek | •Dick Van Dyke |
| •Lou Holtz | •Joe Frazier | •Harmon Killebrew | •Regis Philbin | •Johnny Carson | •Chuck Norris |
| •Davey Johnson | •Arnold Palmer | •Jerry Stackhouse | •Joseph Abboud | •Clint Eastwood | •Arnold Stang |
| •Cal Ripken, Jr. | •Jack Nicklaus | •Andre Agassi | •Bryant Gumbel | •James Earl Jones | •Jerry Orbach |
| •Brady Anderson | •Ben Crenshaw | •Wes Unseld | •Stone Phillips | •Lionel Richie | •Jon Cryer |
| •Rafael Palmeiro | •Johnny Unitas | •Don Scott | •David Hasselhoff | •Art Garfunkle | •Chipper Jones |
| •Roberto Alomar | •Grant Hill | •Richard Sher | •Ted Danson | •John Tesh | •Fred McGriff |
| •Bobby Bonilla | •Ken Kaiser | •Marty Bass | •Jhane Barnes | •Jim Cummings | •Ben Cardin |
| •BJ Surhoff | •Daryl Cousins | •Steve Rouse | •Ed Bradley | •Mark Spitz | •David Schwimmer |

**100% of the proceeds will benefit Chesapeake Habitat for Humanity,** who will select and rehab a home for a deserving Baltimore family. So plan to visit one of our stores and see why these are '*knot*' your average neckties!

### *Gage Downtown*
MONDAY, SEPTEMBER 9 through
SUNDAY, SEPTEMBER 15, 1996

### *Gage Owings Mills*
MONDAY, SEPTEMBER 16 through
SUNDAY, SEPTEMBER 22, 1996

*Both stores closed Saturday, September 14 in observance of the Jewish New Year*

**MENSWEAR SINCE 1946**

*Always World Class. Always Baltimore.*

**DOWNTOWN**
200 W. Baltimore Street
Baltimore, Maryland 21201
(410) 727-0763
M-S 9am-6pm/Sundays 11am - 4pm

**OWINGS MILLS**
9616 Reisterstown Road
Owings Mills, Maryland 21117
(410) 581-5351
M-S 10am-9pm/ Sundays 12pm - 5pm

## How to Get Favorable Media Attention and Publicity: By Being a Flamboyant Character

Yes, there are great risks here—notably the danger of crossing the line from flamboyant to offensive, or at least to "target" status, such as Donald Trump and Martha Stewart in business, or Bill Maher in comedy. However, there are great examples of this gamble paying off big, one of which is big gambler Bob Stupak, who created the Vegas World Hotel and Casino in Las Vegas (now the Stratosphere).

Bob has appeared on *60 Minutes*—in a positive way—been written about in many major newspapers and magazines and hit the national wire services as news at least twice that I know of. His paths to publicity have included inventing and promoting weird casino games, including crapless craps; playing high-stakes poker against a computer; making the largest known bet on a boxing match at a competing casino—and winning; installing the world's largest wheel of fortune; and challenging Donald Trump to a huge wager on one round of the toy-store product *Trump—The Game* (an offer Trump declined).

In the sports world, most people agree that Bill Veeck was the most flamboyant promoter. He's widely credited with inventing "Bat Day" for baseball but is now best remembered for sending a midget up to the plate in a major-league game—thus presenting the pitcher with a strike zone so small as to require surgical precision.

Cal Worthington, a California car dealer, provided late-night TV in his area with truly entertaining commercials, gained national renown, and inspired a host of imitators with his circus animal commercial guest stars, Roy Roger-ish outfits, and wild promises such as, "If you can beat our price, I'll eat a bug!"

In Phoenix, there's a dentist who, once a week, dresses up in a Superman costume and visits school health classes as "Super Dentist," taking along fantastic props including an 8-foot-long toothbrush. Every so often, this flamboyant approach to community service gets him newspaper or TV coverage.

If you want a great case study, consider Jesse Ventura, the former pro wrestler who was elected governor of Minnesota, running as an independent. He shocked both the Republican and Democratic candidates and party leaders. In short order, Jesse pushed through the largest tax cut in that state's history. His quickly written autobiography shot up the bestseller lists. It's hard to be more flamboyant and outrageous than a pro wrestler in bright-colored spandex. More recently, Governor Arnold Schwarzenegger traveled a similar path; he has also transformed himself into a larger-than-life personality.

## How to Get Favorable Media Attention and Publicity: By Being an Expert

The media loves surveys, polls, and statistics. If you commission or conduct some kind of public-opinion or customer-preference study, it'll probably lead to your choice of public media or trade journal exposure for you and your business. A client of mine in the time-management seminar business conducted a survey of top executives from 500 companies, asking them to rate their biggest time-management and productivity problems. Then he compiled the results into a news release and sent it to a variety of magazines, newspapers, and talk shows. He received write-ups in his local newspaper and two business magazines and was interviewed on one radio talk show. Who can copy this idea?

Couldn't a restaurant owner do a survey of dining out and take-home eating habits? Couldn't a florist compile interesting, maybe even humorous data and examples of why men buy roses?

Another certain source of media attention is issuing predictions. Being provocative and predictive attracts the media spotlight as if you were magnetized. One major bank gets tremendous media attention each January when it issues its "economic forecast" for the Phoenix economy in the year ahead.

About eight or nine years ago, I consulted with a group involved in the production of a TV infomercial featuring Joan Quigley, best known (as mentioned earlier) as Nancy Reagan's astrologer. I was in a boardroom with a group of pretty high-powered executives and creative types, working under time pressure to agree on a long list of details about the planned show, but when a brief, casual conversation got Joan started talking about predictions, I can tell you that everybody's ears perked up, the clock-watching was forgotten, and we, too, wanted to know—"What does Joan say?" (which was the title of her book about consulting with the Reagans). People are tirelessly fascinated with predictions!

As you'll probably recall, the radio talk shows were heavily populated with "experts" issuing their predictions about the impending Y2K crisis—and publicizing everything from books to seminars to freeze-dried potato rinds to hideouts in Montana. Being an expert and making predictions is one path to lots of free radio time. There are others, which we'll discuss in a minute.

## How to Get Favorable Media Attention and Publicity: With Creative Promotions

Do you remember the pet rock? As you'll recall, that strange little product got talked about on thousands of radio stations, shown on TV, and written up in newspapers and magazines, providing its inventor with millions of dollars of free advertising. He simply sent pet rocks to the media, and they went nuts over it!

On September 12, 2001, Gold/VIP Member Mitch Carson woke up with the idea of putting Osama bin Laden's face on rolls of toilet paper. The idea quickly spawned a new line of patriotic and anti-terrorist items, from T-shirts to golf balls to dartboards. The medium for sales was a fax campaign to 14,000 gift stores, and more than 150 orders a day poured in. Sales spiked and then died in a brief period but led to interviews with Mitch by FOX News and Reuters Worldwide, a major TV news service—publicity Mitch has leveraged and still uses in his personal promotion as a speaker and consultant, and for his ad specialty and promotional merchandise company, *www.impactproducts.net*.

On a smaller scale, you can generate media interest and coverage with your own unusual products or promotions.

On a Friday the 13th, a record store erected a "superstition obstacle course" in its parking lot—complete with a ladder to walk under, a sidewalk crack to step on, mirrors to break, and a black cat roaming around—and sent dares to all the local radio disc jockeys, newspaper columnists, and TV personalities to go through the obstacle course. One radio station bit and did a live-remote morning drive-time broadcast from the site. Two TV news programs reported it. Thousands of dollars of free advertising resulted.

One of the banks in Phoenix has all its tellers come to work wearing costumes on Halloween—and for three years in a row, they've garnered free advertising on TV news programs with this gimmick.

One of my favorite publicity stunt stories is about a promotion my friend Gary Halbert devised for Tova Borgnine, for the promotion of a new perfume. They ran a big ad (headlined: "Tova Borgnine Swears Under Oath Her New Perfume Contains No Illegal Sexual Stimulants") and offered free samples to the public at a huge "premiere party" at a Los Angeles hotel. The resulting traffic jam and frenzied crowd turned the shamelessly promotional event into a news story that made the TV news, radio news, and the retailing industry news.

## How to Get Free Advertising: As a Guest on Radio Talk Shows

In your area, there are probably a couple of "all talk" radio stations plus other stations with at least one or two talk shows on their daily or weekly schedule. Nationally, there are thousands of such stations. These shows grind up guests at a rapid pace. Their hosts and producers are constantly scrambling to find interesting guests. And there aren't nearly enough celebrities to go around. In fact, 90 percent of all radio talk show guests are ordinary people, virtually unknown to the listening audience before their appearance.

Just about anything we've talked about in this Step can qualify you as a radio talk show guest: an opinion, a prediction, a survey, a study, an opinion poll, a new product, an outrageous promotion, or a charitable activity.

Writing a book is an even surer path to the talk-show microphone, locally or nationally. The book can be your own self-published "consumer guide" dealing with your particular business, or a "real" book published by a "real" publisher, like this one. If you own a restaurant, or chain of restaurants, you could write a book about dining out while on a diet, then appear on radio shows promoting your book and, automatically, also promoting your restaurant. If you have a company that sells educational toys for children, you could write a book about raising superintelligent kids. Oh, and if you think you can't write, hire a ghostwriter to help. A simple classified ad in your local daily or alternative weekly newspaper will bring freelance writers and editors rushing to your door; you also can try posting your needs at *www.e-lance.com*.

If you are a local business owner or professional, appearing on national radio and TV programs and being written about in national publications can make you a big celebrity in your local market—and it can be done! My Platinum Members Bill and Steve Harrison helped their own accountant get interviewed on Lou Dobbs's top-rated financial news program on CNN, which gives him a big "leg up" over other accountants competing for clients in his hometown. If you take a look at a few issues of the Harrisons's publication *Radio/TV Interview Report*, you'll get a lot of ideas of how you might seek fame!

## Resource!

My Platinum Inner Circle Members Bill and Steve Harrison help authors get publicity and get on talk shows through their *Radio/TV Interview Report*, which promotes authors to media outlets, and their National Publicity Summit, where authors meet face-to-face with TV and radio show producers and hosts as well as magazine editors.

Get information at *www.FreePublicity.com* or *www.NationalPublicity Summit.com*. Also, the Harrisons have prepared one of the 12 Course Modules in the 12-Week Ultimate Marketing Plan Course delivered free by e-mail. Enroll at *www.UltimateMarketingPlan.com*.

## The Basic Tools for Getting Free Advertising: The Press Kit and the News Release

A press kit is a folder or booklet of basic information about you; your business, product, or service; your qualifications as an expert; and your background. It can be universally used with any media contact as well as with bankers, lenders, investors, vendors, and even clients or customers. It will typically include some or all of the following:

1. A biographical sketch and/or resume
2. A chronological history of your industry and your business, product, or service
3. Photos of the business, product, or service
4. Photos of you in action with your product or service; you with famous people; you being interviewed on TV, and so on
5. Copies of any articles or excerpts from books you've written
6. Copies of articles about you and your business, product, or service
7. Position statements or press releases—such as those about studies, surveys, polls, new products, nonprofit affiliations, awards received, and other news of interest to the public
8. A list of subjects on which you can be called to comment as a qualified expert

This press kit can be sent with a cover letter to every radio station producer or manager, every TV station producer or manager, every newspaper editor, every magazine editor, individual show hosts and producers, and individual columnists. Your cover letter may suggest a particular reason to schedule you as a guest now or, more generally, suggest that your press kit be kept on file so that you can be called on when they need an expert from your field. Then, periodically, you should mail new information to this same list of targets.

This is usually your first contact with a list you've compiled of media targets who might be interested in you and who could be useful to you. If you become known to these contacts as an interesting, knowledgeable source of information, you will get opportunities!

The other basic tool is a good press release. You can create one press release after another, linking yourself or your business to timely events. Best of all, press releases can be sent via broadcast fax to radio stations and other media at nominal cost.

A world expert in using press releases successfully is my speaking colleague Dr. Paul Hartunian. Paul is the man who actually did sell the Brooklyn Bridge—well, little hunks of it anyway, to the tune of hundreds of thousands of dollars, all via interviews and an 800 number, all created by press releases. For that and other products and businesses, he has been on *The Tonight Show, Oprah, Sally Jesse Raphael,* on CNN, and has even been profiled in *Forbes* magazine. He has generated literally millions of dollars of free yet valuable advertising via simple faxed press releases. One of the biggest points Paul hammers home is that the media are not interested in giving you free advertising, but the media are eager for information and stories that will intrigue, interest, or entertain their readers and viewers.

I have a little personal experience with Paul's point. I got my three *No B.S.* books featured on the prime-time evening news on one of the three networks in Cleveland, one of my home cities, but the station had no interest whatsoever in giving my books free advertising or directly promoting business books. Rather, it was intrigued by the "oddity" of a local resident who raced harness horses, actually drove in the races, and wrote business books. So, I was interviewed by the sports reporter, not the business reporter. I was in my racing colors, standing next to a horse.

But the books were nicely displayed on bales of straw and shown in the segment, which aired twice. Mission accomplished.

_____ **Resource!** _____

You'll find free information about publicity and news releases from Paul Hartunian at *www.Hartunian.com*. Steve Harrison helps people prepare to meet the media, interest reporters and producers in their stories, and do well on radio and TV programs. Get information from Steve at *www.FreePublicity.com*.

# Malibuism—Becoming Hot

MESSAGE

MARKET

MEDIA

Shortly after moving to Arizona in 1978, I went through a divorce and found myself single and "in the market"—and at that time, the market was Thursday, Friday, and Saturday nights at one place and one place only: an incredibly popular nightclub called Bogart's. Anybody who was anybody frequented Bogart's. All the beautiful people frequented Bogart's. In a city of three-quarters of a million people, there might as well have been only one nightclub. The line to get in the front door was often a hundred people long, but if you "knew somebody" you could be granted the great and glorious privilege of buying a $100.00 membership card entitling you to enter via the line at the back door, which was often shorter.

I was there on a Thursday night when it was as I've just described. But that same Saturday, I returned to find a nearly empty Bogart's. "What happened?" I asked the bartender. "Did they drop the bomb and forget to tell me?"

He shrugged his shoulders and said, "When you're hot you're hot, when you're not you're not."

Bogart's never got hot again. Only a short time later, it ceased to exist. You sure can go from hot to cold in a hurry.

> **ULTIMATE MARKETING SIN #3**
> **Taking Your Customer's Loyalty for Granted**

## Fads and Trends

The entire American automobile industry nearly put itself out of business by stubbornly, stupidly *assuming* that Americans wouldn't buy Japanese cars. Network TV has lost one-third of its viewers and is now frantically trying to recover; the people who run it sat around and said, people will never pay to watch better TV programming.

Once upon a time there was buy-American loyalty. There was brand-name loyalty. There was neighborhood-merchant loyalty. Once upon a time. Today, you've got to keep getting hot all over again.

California may very well be the fad capital of America. Consider the rising and falling fortunes of EST and primal scream therapy . . . women's underwear becoming outerwear . . . the Beverly Hills diet . . . injections of sheep sperm. Malibu-ites can afford to indulge their every whim—they have plenty of 'em—and some whim-satisfiers make fortunes for their creators.

But California has no exclusive on all this. Tragically, young boys in all the inner cities of America have been assaulted, mugged, and occasionally even killed by others desperate for their designer-name sneakers. Even in Kansas, Austin Powers was BIG. Malibu-ism invades even Tupelo.

## The Father of the Fad Everybody Remembers

On April Fool's Day, 1975, advertising man Gary Dahl dropped into his favorite tavern for a beer, got involved with a group talking about their pets, and when asked if he had a pet, replied: "You bet, I've got a pet that's perfectly housebroken, cheap to feed, loyal, and easy to take care of and that knows tricks. In fact, he can roll over and play dead better than any other pet in the world."

"Yeah? What kind of pet is that?"

"My pet rock," Gary said, and the group broke into laughter. Pretty soon, the group was enthusiastically involved in coming up with all the best things about having a pet rock. Gary listened. Then he went home and spent a couple of weeks at the typewriter coming up with the funny owner's manual to go with the pet rock.

One year later, Gary was a bona fide millionaire.

Since then, thousands of people have sought fast wealth through inventing fads; few have been successful. But a surer path to wealth is to adopt the principles behind the incredible success of the pet rock to ordinary products, services, or businesses . . . over and over and over again.

## The New, Short Product Life Cycles

Way back in 1996, Ken Hakuta, known as "Dr. Fad," raised the issue of short product life cycles—which I prefer to call "short customer interest cycles." Ken made his first fortune in 1982, with the sticky-footed, wall-climbing octopus toys called Wall Walkers. He sold nearly 150 million of those goofy things. Ken has his M.B.A. from Harvard, but he's never been a traditional marketer. He advised, "Pretend you're marketing to kids. They get bored with products easily and outgrow them. A company must constantly develop new ideas and be agile enough to turn them into working products—fast."

Ken observed that today's adults are acting more like kids than they used to. He astutely recognized the marketplace impact of declining attention spans and abbreviated interest cycles. This is truer than ever. These days, people have the attention span of gnats.

This behavioral trend has been helped along by the little device known as the remote control. And the trend is most easily observed while watching anybody watching TV with a remote in hand. What does that person do? You bet: click up and down, up and down, station to station. Bore people for even a second and they're gone!

It might interest you to know that men zap about four times more than women, and, conversely, women are four times more likely to click to a program and then stay there until the end than are men. This may be wired in. It's possible that males are born with an attention deficit disorder gene women don't have. It is activated by wedding vows, then stimulated repeatedly by the insertion of any small object into the hand. To any women reading: The next time he dozes off in front of the tube, gently take the remote out of his hand, and gently replace it with a flashlight; when he awakes, he'll click away for five or ten minutes before figuring out the problem!

Actually, my theory is that this little clicker is the last thing we men have any control over in the household, so by God, we're gonna use it.

Anyway, that noise you hear in a quiet neighborhood at night ain't crickets. Research from various sources, averaged together, suggests the average TV viewer "zaps" every two to three minutes. Could there be any greater evidence of the disintegration of attention span? Now, DVR and TiVO are popular because they let people skip commercials, and advertisers are trying to find different ways to use TV. For example, paid product placements in shows are way up. But whether you're presenting a TV infomercial or a direct-mail piece or a print ad long on copy, you have to be very conscious of the need to keep "re-interesting" the customer minute by minute.

This is sort of like the "pull 'em back in" factor I talk about in the companion book to this one *(The Ultimate Sales Letter)* with regard to printed marketing materials.

This extends from the living room and TV to the sales letter in the mail, to the Web site on the Internet, to the aisle in the store. Your customers are impatient, easily bored "zappers."

## How Not to Get Zapped

Possibly the biggest underlying secret to Gary Dahl's Pet Rock was *fun*. Everybody had fun with it. It wasn't the rock; it was the idea—carried out in the owner's manual—that made it all fun.

Ken Hakuta said, "Colgate came out with a toothpaste pump first, and Crest had to play follow-the-leader. But who's to say that the pump is any better than the tube? The important thing is that it's different. In my fad marketing strategy, the pump would be only the first of many changes. A year later I might introduce different flavors; after that, toothpaste dispensed from an aerosol can; then a bubblegum toothpaste . . . well, you get the idea."

You bet. The idea is:

> **ULTIMATE MARKETING SECRET WEAPON #9**
> **Constant Change**

We are so interested in the new and different, we express it in vernacular. When we greet someone, we say, "What's *new?*" We *don't* ask, "Hey, what's old? What's the same as it was the last time I ran into you?" Why don't we ask that? Because we just don't care about what's old.

If you want to keep your customers, keep your customers interested, and keep getting your customers to tell others about you, you've got to keep coming up with good answers to the question, "What's new?"

During what insiders refer to as "the dark ages" after Walt's death, the Disney empire was crumbling—because there was nothing new going on. Eventually, Michael Eisner came in and re-created the magic of constant, almost frantic, certainly frenetic innovation, and the fortunes of the Disney business machine have never been brighter.

Probably the best example, though, is McDonald's. Hardly a two-week period passes without something new or something different going on at McDonald's: a new product, an incredible offer, a new game, a new free gift. "We can invent," Ray Kroc once said, "faster than the others can copy," and that they do. So should you.

## Seven Ways to Get Hot and Keep Getting Hot All Over Again

Here are things you can do to make sure you're not left behind by quick-changing consumers.

### 1. Get Prestigious Recognition

Chances are, your local newspaper or entertainment magazine publishes an annual or semiannual "Best of (your city's name)" issue. You have publications with columnists, radio shows with hosts, TV shows with reporters that all need to be wooed by you—they do have influence in your market! Having well-known people patronize your business and having the media talking about your business makes everybody else want to join the "in crowd."

If you market within an industry niche, rather than to the general public, there's less media, but its publishers and editors tend to be more accessible. In 1997, my client Joe Polish of Piranha Marketing was named "CleanFax Man of the Year" and was featured on that carpet cleaning industry trade journal's front cover in a striking double photo; Joe in a devil's cape with horns, and Joe as an angel with a halo, symbolizing his controversial reputation in the industry. The magazine featured a full-length, favorable profile. He has since made massive, profitable use of reprints of that article. In fact, a full eight years afterward, he is still getting mileage out of these reprints! But this didn't happen by happy accident. Over a couple years prior to this "recognition," Joe carefully and aggressively cultivated a very good relationship with the publisher of the magazine. He interviewed the publisher for his own monthly audiocassette series; he frequently mentioned the magazine in his own newsletter; he invited the publisher to his seminars; he even helped the publisher with a direct-mail campaign. He kept in constant touch with this publisher, occasionally calling just to swap ideas.

## 2. Seek Out New Products

Voraciously read trade magazines, business magazines, and newspapers—and frequently attend conventions, expos, and trade shows in search of interesting, exciting new products you can offer to your customers.

## 3. Develop New Services

Find new, different, and better ways to be of service to your customers.

## 4. Tie into Trends and News Events

Get involved with what people are thinking and talking about. One of the great direct-response copywriters of all time, Robert Collier, talked about "entering the conversation already taking place in the prospect's mind." This is a powerful strategy, requiring considerable insight and understanding of your market, awareness of what's going on in their lives and in the news, and opportunistic action.

When Bill Gates came under attack by the government for monopolistic, unfair business practices, and every day's news was reporting on that, one of my clients alertly added copy to his ads, sales letters, and faxes talking about how using his product would give your business such an unfair advantage you'd destroy and dominate your competitors just like Bill Gates did, but without having to testify or pay huge fines. Response to his advertising went up by nearly 50 percent.

Shortly after the first election of Bill Clinton, when Hillary was put in charge of the national health-care scheme, it was easy to demonize her amongst conservatives. In one client's full-page magazine ad for a financial opportunity, I added a "P.S." paragraph just mentioning Hillary coming to take away a lot of your money to pay for everybody else's cradle-to-grave health care, and suggested that you needed to get rich fast, before it was too late. The response to the ad increased significantly.

When the first Iraq war, Desert Storm, was ending, I noticed an article in a trade journal reporting on a surge in Frederick's of Hollywood's sales, apparently stimulated by the wives and girlfriends of soldiers preparing for homecoming celebrations. I clipped it and sent it to an acquaintance of mine who owns two lingerie stores in a "military town." She did a quick welcome-home theme mailing, announcing a special sale, to her customer list as well as to a rented list of military households. She got huge response.

## 5. Tie into Seasons and Holidays

Again, get involved with what people are thinking and talking about! Here's a partial list of seasons and special days you might tie a promotion to:

| | |
|---|---|
| January/Week 1 | New Year |
| January/Week 3 | Martin Luther King Day |
| January/Week 4 | Australia Day |
| February/Week 1 | Start promoting for Valentine's Day |
| February/Week 2 | Lincoln's Birthday |
| February/Week 3 | Washington's Birthday |

| | |
|---|---|
| March/Weeks 1 to 3 | St. Patrick's Day |
| March/Week 3 or 4 | Spring officially begins |
| April/Week 1 | April Fool's Day |
| April/Weeks 2 and 3 | Easter |
| April/Week 4 | Italian Liberation Week |
| May/Weeks 1 to 3 | Mother's Day |
| May/Week 3 | Armed Forces Day |
| May/Week 5 | Memorial Day |
| June/Week 3 | Flag Day |
| June/Week 4 | Summer officially begins |
| | Father's Day |
| July/Week 1 | Fourth of July |
| July/Weeks 2 to 4 | Peak of summer—all summer activities |
| August/Weeks 3, 4, and 5 | Back-to-School readiness |
| September/Week 1 | Labor Day |
| September/Weeks 4 and 5 | Rosh Hashanah, Yom Kippur |
| September/Week 5 | Autumn officially begins |
| October/Week 2 | Columbus Day |
| October/Weeks 3, 4, and 5 | Halloween |
| November/Weeks 1 and 2 | Election Day |
| November/Week 3 | Veteran's Day |
| November/Weeks 1, 2, and 3 | Thanksgiving |
| November/Weeks 3 and 4 | Inauguration of holiday shopping season |
| December/All Weeks | Christmas and Hanukkah |
| December/All Weeks | Winter activities |
| December/Weeks 3 and 4 | New Year's Eve |

As you can see, there's hardly a week that goes by that you can't be starting, in the throes of, or winding up, a seasonal or holiday-related promotion for your business. You can also find lists of obscure holidays in books at the library or bookstore, if a lighter, humorous touch is appropriate for your business.

## 6. Tie into Movies and Entertainment Events

An awful lot of water-cooler and coffee-klatch conversation has to do with the TV shows of the night before, the movies seen over the weekend, and gossip about celebrities. As I was writing this edition of this book, ABC's *Desperate Housewives* was the hottest of the hottest of the things on TV. Everybody watching, everybody talking about it. In my *No B.S. Marketing Letter*, I took a massage therapy clinic's coupon-flyer and gave it a complete makeover with a Desperate Housewives theme. (If you'd like to see it, enroll in the 12-Week Ultimate Marketing Plan Course, free, at *www.UltimateMarketingPlan.com*.)

A very successful fundraising event that a friend and I helped develop for a local chapter of the Arthritis Foundation was an Oscars party, held at Planet Hollywood the night the Oscar Awards are televised. For as long as I can remember, bars have used Monday Night Football as an event. In my travels, I saw an Italian restaurant advertising a Sunday night Sopranos event, with dinner, live music, and the *Sopranos* TV show on big screen TVs.

*TV Guide* may hold the clues to your next event, too.

## 7. Piggyback on Others' Fads, Even If They Are Unrelated

I don't know about you, but if they had come to me and invited me to invest in a movie about giant turtles who lived in the sewers, ate pizza, sang rock music, and were martial arts experts, I would have whipped my checkbook right out. Sure. Nevertheless, the *Teenage Mutant Ninja Turtles* were big, big, big! And Pizza Hut astutely latched onto their coattails—uh, shells.

But Pizza Hut didn't own this opportunity. A dentist I know went out and bought some stuffed Teenage Mutant Ninja Turtles, displayed them in his office, and mailed all his patients this offer: bring in any child for a special $9.95 exam and he or she can take home the turtle of his or her choice—while supplies last—free!

If I had owned a pet store—or a record store, a toy store, or a kids' shoe store—I can guarantee you that I would have run some kind of green promotion the year the Turtles got hot.

Fortunately, there's some kind of comparable fad every few months or so. Before the ink is dry on the pages of this book, whatever examples I might mention could be distant memory, but another opportunity will have presented itself for astute marketers to capitalize on.

## Fantastic Examples

I want to tell you about three great examples from 2004.

First up is the Ketchup Wars promotion, developed by my client Rory Fatt at Restaurant Marketing Systems, and used by restaurant owners nationwide.

Piggybacking on Teresa Heinz Kerry and the U.S. presidential election, an entrepreneur began marketing a brand of ketchup labeled "W," for Republicans who couldn't bear to put Heinz ketchup on their Freedom Fries! Rory piggybacked on that product, helping restaurant owners use the two brands as a means of polling customers. Customers indicated their presidential choice by choice of ketchup, the restaurants reported the results to ketchupwars.com, and news releases were sent to media outlets. Hundreds of restaurant owners got publicity in their local newspapers and on radio and TV programs. One restaurant was the subject of a report during prime-time TV news, with promotional plugs all night long, including during the season premiere of the popular show *Law and Order.*

Second, my Gold/VIP Member Lester Nathan, an advertising and business consultant to independent pharmacy owners, gets kudos for rapid response to a timely news event. His ad, shown as Exhibit #11, was prepared for his pharmacy clients and running in newspapers within thirty-six hours of the first news of the arthritis drug Vioxx being pulled from the marketplace by the FDA.

**Exhibit #11**

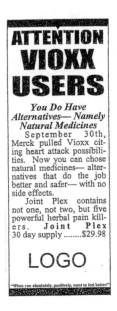

Third, Platinum Member Chauncey Hutter Jr., a marketing advisor for tax preparers and accountants, did a little pro bono work for his church, and wrote a sales letter headlined:

### "WHO ELSE WANTS ANSWERS ABOUT GOD
### AFTER SEEING THE PASSION OF CHRIST?"

**Local Business Owner Speaks Out**
**about Controversial Movie**

You can see his entire letter in one of the installments of the free 12-Week Ultimate Sales Letter Course delivered by e-mail, available at *www.UltimateMarketingPlan.com*.

Because news events are shorter-lived today than ever before, many opportunities that occur require very rapid response on your part. Fortunately, you have access to fast-response media, which will be discussed in Step 12.

# "Poor Boy" Marketing Strategies

MESSAGE

MARKET

MEDIA

Early in my business career, I was wisely advised, "Boy, the first thing you got to do is avoid going broke while you're getting rich and famous." Had I paid closer attention, I might very well have saved myself from considerable financial strife. Observing others, I've noticed how frequently entrepreneurs bankrupt themselves with expensive advertising and marketing schemes when their interests would be better served by low-cost methods. When you stop to think about it, it's easy to "buy customers"—given enough money (or credit), any idiot can build up a business, and many idiots have, using up millions of dollars of stockholders' equity in the process. Genius is in getting customers and making sales without having to use up a huge chunk of capital to do it. The ideas in this chapter are dedicated to that objective.

## It's Opportunity Calling!

The phone rang persistently in the little shoe store where I was buying a pair of shoes. Finally, after six rings, the clerk at the counter said, "Dammit—I'm busy" but grudgingly answered the phone. Guess how he sounded to the caller?

This attitudinal error must occur a million times a day in every imaginable type of business, as the incoming call "interrupts" the important work. Fix this and you've taken a giant step forward in attracting new customers as well as retaining the ones you have.

An inbound call can be many things: the tax collector, your mother-in-law announcing a surprise two-week visit, or the merchant next door reporting that your roof is on fire. These calls have varying degrees of importance. But the call can be and often is from a prospective customer, present customer, or past customer, and that is Opportunity calling! These calls must not be thought of as interruptions.

If the call is from a prospective customer, the job of the person handling the call must be clearly defined, understood, and enthusiastically pursued: to get the customer into the store, to get her name, address, and phone number, or to set up an appointment. It is not just to dispense information.

Let me tell you one of the most instructive true marketing stories I have ever encountered:

The owner of a large auto-parts store was extraordinarily frustrated with his advertising, complaining about weekly expenditures of tens of thousands of dollars in the newspaper, on radio, and on television, all yielding few customers. But a conversation with his employees revealed their frustration with the constant ringing of the phone—calls from people asking questions, constantly interrupting them. A Saturday in his store provided a count of more than 200 incoming calls. Here's how every one was handled, with varying levels of courtesy and friendliness:

"XYZ Auto Parts—how can we help you?" The caller would then state his business. Most often, his inquiry sounded like this: "I saw (heard) your ad—how much is a flibittygibbet for a '68 Ford?"

The answer then went like this: "Lemme look it up—hold on . . . still there? It's sixty-two fifty." Click.

As you can immediately detect, there was no problem at all with this guy's advertising. And, to be fair, his people really weren't at fault either. He was the problem. He was the one who had no earthly idea what was going on inside his own business. He was the one who had failed to educate his people about the importance of these calls. He was the one who had failed to train his people in effective handling of the calls. He was the one who had failed to motivate his people. He was the one who had failed to monitor their performance.

Here's what we did:

1. We devised a new phone script to capture the caller's name, address, and number.
2. We taught the script to all the employees.
3. We instituted a reward pool of fifty cents per captured name, address, and phone number, divided at day's end by everybody working that day.
4. We added a "telephone upsell" to the script.

## ULTIMATE MARKETING SECRET WEAPON #10
### Capture Callers' Identity and Market to Them

Immediately, with this strategy, the number of callers converted—ones who came into the store that same day—increased significantly. Overall, after follow-up mailings to all the callers, the store captured more than 50 percent of the callers as customers!

## ULTIMATE MARKETING SECRET WEAPON #11
### The Telephone Upsell

In addition, we added revenue and profit with the telephone upsell.

You're familiar with this if you've ever ordered by phone from a well-run catalog company. After the operator has taken your order, she'll usually do a "Columbo": Oh, just one more thing. We have a special offer just for today's callers—would you like to hear about it? I recently ordered from The Sharper Image, and the operator walked me through six different specials.

This technique works in that application, and there's no reason it can't work in others.

The auto-parts store's upsell script sounded like this:

"Oh, just one more thing—we have an extra special offer just for today's callers—would you like to hear about it?"

More than 70 percent said yes.

"Good. Any caller who comes in today or by noon tomorrow will receive a 5 percent discount coupon good for any purchase in the store and a free copy of our 400-page catalog. Also, there's a sale right now on (insert product). I can set your coupon and catalog aside in your name if you are coming in. Should I do that?"

More than 50 percent said yes. More than 25 percent actually showed up. More than 15 percent not only came in but also bought the item they originally called to ask about and bought the sale item described on the phone.

## Reach Out and Grab a Customer

Fact: the telephone lines run in both directions, in and out. According to Bernie Goldberg, author of the book *How to Manage and Executive Telephone Selling*, someone making outbound telemarketing calls to homes can average twenty-five to thirty-five dialings per hour and ten to fifteen completed calls per hour; someone calling businesses, twenty to thirty dialings and five to ten completed calls per hour. If a person costs you $10.00 per hour and completes just five calls, that's a cost of $2.00 per presentation; if the person gets ten done, you're down to a cost of $1.00 per presentation. This is comparable to or less than other advertising and marketing methods and much faster to get done.

Why use the telephone? Well, just about everybody's got one. And just about everybody answers it when it rings. They may skip your ad in the newspaper. They may throw out your mail unopened. But when the phone rings, they answer.

My appreciation for the phone goes back to age fifteen (yes—fifteen!) when I decided to make some money selling Amway products. My parents were distributors, and I have to say, as an aside, that the exposure to selling, to certain attitudes, and to ambitious people that I received thanks to their involvement was, and is, priceless.

Having no money for advertising, no car to get around in, and no friends, relatives, or neighbors to sell to—those were my parents' customers—I was left with the telephone and the white pages. With some help, I devised a little telephone survey beginning with questions about environmental and water-pollution concerns, then switching to a pitch for Amway's biodegradable, ecologically wonderful, etc., laundry compound. Even the fuzziness of the passing of time has not blurred the memory of how miserable it was to make these calls: hundreds and hundreds of no answers, hundreds of people too old, too young, unable to speak English, or unbelievably nasty, and hours without a positive response. But I also clearly remember the "thrill of victory." And, more important, I can look back and realize that with a lousy script, terrible technique, and no selectivity in prospects, I still made money and acquired customers. I left that business more than thirty-three years ago, but I happen to know that some of those customers are still buying Amway products today, month after month after month, each having cumulatively spent tens of thousands of dollars.

Sadly, such "cold" telephone prospecting to consumers is now outlawed. However, you can use postcards, sales letters, ads, Web sites, and every other medium to motivate people to call you or call your "free recorded message" (see Step 12); then, with their permission, you can make follow-up calls to them. Telephone conversation with interested prospects remains one of the most direct, cost-effective marketing tools available to us.

An interesting substitute is the "tele-seminar" or "tele-conference" to which prospects are invited as a group (also discussed in Step 12).

Now, for some good news: there are basically no restrictions on business-to-business telemarketing.

For a printing company, I had a list compiled of small businesses and phone numbers from the area immediately surrounding the shop, created a simple phone script, and made a competition out of it for the five employees, none of whom were salespeople or telemarketers. They each "found the time" to make one call per hour—eight calls per day. The one who got the most new customers during the week got $100.00. The shop made 40 calls a day, 200 calls a week for $100.00—fifty cents each. The shop also gained an average of ten new customers each week. ANY business could copy this idea.

Some years ago, Fran Tarkenton, former NFL superstar turned businessman, with whom I had the pleasure of coauthoring "The Be Your Own Boss System" for *Entrepreneur Magazine* and with whom I've worked on two TV infomercials, got the idea of selling advertising space on airline ticket jackets. He struck a deal with an airline, then faced a question: How best to get the advertisers under contract?

Fran chose the simplest, cheapest, fastest way he could think of: He locked himself in a New York City hotel room for several days and called prospects on the phone. The strength of his name was enough to get through to decision-makers; other marketers have to find other ways to get that done. In less than a week, Fran sold millions of dollars of advertising contracts for his newly invented medium to major national corporations and made himself a lot of money.

There is one overwhelmingly superior way most businesses should use telemarketing, if they use it only one way:

## ULTIMATE MARKETING SECRET WEAPON #12
### Telemarketing after Direct Mail

Almost without exception, a telemarketing campaign linked to direct mail increases the initial direct-mail results by 500 to 1,000 percent!

Here's a formula for a telemarketing script that is simple and effective:

1.  IDENTIFY YOURSELF
    This is John Smith from ABC Widgets calling.

2.  REASON FOR CALLING
    I'm calling to arrange for delivery of a free gift for the person in your company responsible for purchasing widgets.
    OR
    I'm calling to follow up on my letter to the person in charge of purchasing widgets, to arrange for delivery of a free gift.

3.  IDENTIFY DECISION-MAKER
    Who in your company handles widget purchasing?

4. GET TO THE DECISION-MAKER

   May I speak to Mr. Widget Buyer for just three minutes please?

5. GET PAST "SCREENING"

   Rather than leaving my name and number, I'd very much appreciate setting a time that I should call back—I need to arrange for delivery of his gift with him personally within two days. (ALTERNATIVE CLOSE) Would it be better if I called back at (insert time) or (insert time)?

6. REPEAT 1 AND 2 WITH DECISION-MAKER

   Mr. Widget Buyer, I'm John Smith from ABC Widgets. As part of our (insert month) new-customer promotion, your company has been selected to receive, as a free gift (insert whatever the gift is), just for (insert desired result: coming into store this week, setting up an appointment, whatever) and I'm calling to arrange for you to receive this gift.

7. ASK FOR THE DESIRED ACTION

   Example: I'd like to personally bring your gift in and give you a brief demonstration of the ABC Widget in action. Would tomorrow morning or afternoon be better for you?
   OR
   Example: I'd like to set your gift aside with your name on it, but I have to know when you'll be coming in. Will tomorrow morning or afternoon be better for you?

## YCDBSOYA

My father had a pair of cufflinks when I was a kid that were black squares with raised gold letters: YCDBSOYA. The letters stand for:

## You Can't Do Business Sitting On Your Ass

A few years ago, a favorite restaurant of mine failed during its "summer slump." But at no time did its owners get up off their butts and go out into the community door-to-door to hand out coupons or flyers. Or go to the phone and make telemarketing calls. Or do anything else that was proactive. They just sat there and the business died.

In the same community, that same summer, a young chiropractor got ready to open his new practice—with at least a dozen competing chiropractors surrounding his office already established in the area. He spent one full month prior to opening going door-to-door, house-to-house, introducing himself, asking the residents about the area and their health interests, and making friends. He knocked on more than 2,000 doors that month. And from the first day he started seeing patients, his practice has prospered. In its first year, it outperformed all the established practices in the area.

There are three types of people: those who make things happen, those who watch things happen, and those who wonder what happened. I think you'll find that most successful businesspeople you know are in the first category.

# Through the Looking Glass

Bruce David, a savvy marketing consultant, told me about the hardware store owner located in a busy shopping center. The owner white-painted almost all of his window, leaving open only a small circle that passersby could look through. Above the circle, he posted a sign reading *FOR MEN'S EYES ONLY.*

Inside, Bruce and the storeowner had constructed an impressive display of power tools along with signs featuring great sale prices.

As you can imagine, people lined up to peer through the circle. Very few people passed without looking. People who would have passed an ordinary window display without a second glance were drawn to this display. And, in case you were wondering, just as many women looked as did men.

If you own any kind of retail establishment and can't "steal" this idea, you're brain dead. I am continually amazed at the number of businesspeople who do not use their windows to promote and to attract customers.

Here are some other great window ideas:

- "Live" mannequins
- Big-screen TVs playing videos
- Weird objects, like The World's Largest Ball of Barbed Wire
- Huge objects. A company in New York called THINK BIG, INC. offers giant pencils, crayons, toothbrushes, baseball gloves, and dozens of other objects perfect for store-window displays.

## Teaser Advertising

The problem with running a big ad in the newspaper, in a trade journal, or in a national magazine is the number of people you pay for who simply don't see it. On any one day, your best prospects may be out of town, sick in bed, or too busy to read the newspaper.

One strategy to focus attention on your big ad is to precede it with a series of tiny, low-cost teaser ads. For example, consider the new computer store desirous of making the business community aware of its existence. For two months, in the weekly city business journal, it ran these small display ads:

COMING ON THIS PAGE IN 4 WEEKS:

THE MOST ADVANCED ...

COMING ON THIS PAGE IN 3 WEEKS:

THE MOST ADVANCED SOLUTIONS ...

COMING ON THIS PAGE IN 2 WEEKS:

THE MOST ADVANCED SOLUTIONS TO 46 DIFFERENT . . .

COMING ON THIS PAGE IN JUST 1 WEEK:

THE MOST ADVANCED SOLUTIONS TO 46 DIFFERENT

NAGGING, FRUSTRATING, EXPENSIVE BUSINESS

PROBLEMS PLUS 1 ABSOLUTELY IRRESISTIBLE FREE

GIFT OFFER . . .

By the time the computer store ran its full-page grand-opening advertisement, including suggested computer solutions to forty-six problems and a
great free-gift offer, the regular readers of this journal *were looking for his ad.*

## Chug, Chug, Chug Advertising

One of the tele-conferences I did last year was with Platinum Member
Jerry Jones and Gold/VIP Member Derek Freund on "Direct Mail Secrets."
Both these guys mail hundreds of thousands—even millions—of direct-
mail pieces each year for their clients, so they have a wealth of knowledge.
One of the things we talked about is the business owner's discipline in
finding and continuing to use the "bread-'n'-butter" methods of bringing in customers . . . those things that aren't flashy, that don't produce
huge numbers, but just chug along month after month, earning their
keep. There are those things in direct mail. There are such things in print
advertising as well.

Most businesses *can* utilize small and, in some media, inexpensive
ads that target specific prospects, and earn their keep continuously—but
most businesses *don't.*

One good example is the small ads in the *New Yorker* magazine.
If you read the *New Yorker, Atlantic Monthly,* or a number of other

"high-end demographic" magazines, you will see many ads like these, including many appearing every month, unchanged, year after year after year. Nothing fancy. Nothing real smart. Yet most of these are effective enough to keep running. For your own education, you might go to the library, pick up a dozen diverse magazines—*Esquire, Rolling Stone, Cosmo, Entrepreneur, Popular Mechanics*—and find these little ads in the current month's issue. Then look at an issue of the same magazines from two, three, or five years ago to see how many small ads in those old issues match the current ones. You'll probably be surprised at the number.

Admittedly, one small ad does not a business make. But my friend Melvin Powers at Wilshire Books built a huge mail-order book business with ads this size run month after month, year after year, in hundreds of magazines. Each keeps chugging along, producing small numbers but producing sufficient numbers. Combined, they produce big numbers. Gold/VIP Member Dr. Paul Searby fueled his very profitable dental assistant school exclusively with small classified ads only in weekly community newspapers in a circle around his office. One of my private clients, who prefers I not use him or his ads as examples, has run the same two-inch display ad in some eight or nine magazines for more than ten years, and makes a very comfortable living doing nothing else.

This is a rather dull and boring approach, so most don't stick with the program! For example, one client had a two-inch ad he was running in four or five of his industry's trade journals. Some months he was also in those same magazines with full-page ads; in other months he was not. Over six months, the dinky ads produced a 5-to-1 return on investment (ROI). But he stopped running them. You might ask: Why? For one thing, the ROI was healthy but the numbers unexciting—forty or fifty leads, eight to ten sales. For another, he was bored with them. This occurs with a lot of people. They are too impatient to put a lot of "little vending machines" in offbeat locations, each selling one bottle of goo a week—they want the one big "store" that'll attract thousands. They lack the discipline to keep tiny ads running in many publications every month. However, the longevity of businesses deriving little streams of profitable businesses from many different places is better and more certain than those businesses deriving big floods from few sources.

There's a lot to be said for "grinding it out." I just returned from Vegas. Most people would be surprised to know the very small number of profit dollars produced per hour by each slot machine, by each table game. The casinos really do "grind out" small dollars multiplied by lots of machines. In fact, the lingo for the down 'n' dirty, slots-only places is "grind joint."

A worthy goal is development and ownership of a small, "evergreen" ad that can just chug along, week or month after week or month, year after year. I envy those who own such incredibly valuable assets pretty much ignored by competition. The ad for shoe lifts to make men taller, for example, has run every month in a number of magazines for at least thirty-five years that I'm aware of, without one word changed. Wish it were mine.

The Internet has made this approach more viable. In an increasing number of arenas, it is economically feasible to use these small ads to drive interested prospects to a Web site and to offer no other means of response—something I would have argued vehemently against two years ago but now know works in certain situations. In fact, I will soon be testing it myself for a particular product.

Why not find as many places as you can to run a little ad, constantly? Do this even if one place makes only $1.00 profit every month.

## Take-One Boxes and Contest-Entry Boxes

Everything from cosmetic makeovers and spa memberships to vacation clubs and credit cards are successfully promoted via take-one boxes and contest-entry boxes placed in businesses.

The purpose of these box systems is, of course, to collect names of somewhat qualified prospects for follow-up by mail or phone. A box can cost as little as a couple of dollars and, located in a busy business, collect hundreds of leads each week. A retail business that I had an interest in for several years had its managers drop off contest-entry boxes at outdoor bank ATM machines on Friday evenings and pick them up Sunday evenings to collect hundreds and hundreds of leads for follow-up. The banks probably would not have approved of this gambit, but I will tell you it was very effective.

A couple of years ago, I worked with a company marketing home security and fire protection systems by bringing homeowners to group presentations at local restaurants, as winners of free dinners. They got all their leads from contest-entry boxes placed (with permission, unlike the above-mentioned guerilla use of ATM locations) in gas stations, convenience stores, other retail stores, beauty salons, and so on, all over each town where the company had sales reps.

If I had a business that could effectively follow up on leads by mail or phone, I would develop a contest-entry box and hire a reliable, ambitious college student in need of extra income to place a number of the boxes and then service them weekly or biweekly. I would pay the kid by the number of leads or the number of leads converted to appointments or customers.

When using a contest-entry box system, it's important to offer and honestly deliver a valuable, appealing first prize. In Phoenix, weekend getaways to cooler San Diego work very well. But, although not announced in advance, every entrant wins a second prize.

Let's say you want to promote an Italian restaurant, and you want to specifically increase your weekday early dinner traffic. First, you get ten contest-entry boxes placed in nonrestaurant businesses, probably in a circle around your restaurant. Second, you collect all the leads after a week or two. Third, you or somebody else calls these leads, or you send mail to these leads with this message:

> Thank you for entering our San Diego vacation contest. Unfortunately, you did not win the first prize—it was won by Mr. and Mrs. Jones of Glendale, Arizona. However, you have won a valuable second prize: The enclosed certificate entitles you and your spouse or friend to a 2-for-1 dinner deal at our beautiful Italian Ristorante on 12th

Street, Monday through Thursday from 5:00 P.M. to 7:30 P.M. With this certificate, you pay for just 1 dinner and get a 2nd dinner of equal or lesser value free! Enclosed is a miniature copy of our menu so you can see in advance the tremendous variety and reasonable prices we offer. Please call for reservations and redeem your certificate within the next 21 days.

If nothing else, these strategies dispel the damaging, often repeated idea that you need money to make money. I was recently at a seminar where each attendee's business project was analyzed, discussed, and worked on by the entire group. One fellow came there with the belief that he needed to raise or borrow $2 million to successfully implement his business project. By the time the seminar was over, he had a good business plan requiring less than $5,000.00.

## The Power of Cooperation

Cooperation can be carried too far, a camel being a horse built by committee, and I am not a big fan of groups. But I do believe in strategic alliances.

> **ULTIMATE MARKETING SECRET WEAPON #13**
> **Asset Sharing for Marketing Success**

Two noncompeting but somehow related merchants—such as a pet store owner and a veterinarian; a restaurant owner and a theater owner; a sporting goods store owner and a sports-bar proprietor; an auto dealer and a car wash owner; a computer company and an office supply store—can share their customer bases, their store traffic, and even their advertising to build each others' businesses and stretch their advertising dollars.

In this same category of cooperation, there are joint ventures. In the world, there are basically just two groups: those with customers and those without customers. Each has a need, although someone in the first group must often be educated by someone in the second. The person with a thriving business and good group of responsive customers needs to be of greater and greater service to those customers, and he needs ways to make more money with his customers without doing more work. He may or may not understand this, but he owns the most valuable asset in the world: customers. Then there's you—the entrepreneur with a product or service or business that would be of interest and value to his customers. In direct marketing terms, he could be a "host" and you could be a beneficial "parasite."

Simple example: A dry cleaner has 500 good, repeat customers. But he's nearly at capacity and couldn't do much more dry-cleaning work without adding equipment and space and personnel. How can he make more money? Well, those 500 customers have carpets in their homes, and two or three times a year, they need a good, reliable carpet cleaner. Mr. Dry Cleaner isn't prone to get into a second business. But you, Mr. Carpet Cleaner, can pay him for an introduction and endorsement to his customers. That's host/parasite marketing.

The absolute all-time master of this in my kind of business, the information products and seminar business, is my Platinum Inner Circle Member Ted Thomas, an expert in teaching tax lien, real estate, and foreclosure investing strategies. Ted sells millions of dollars' worth of his books, courses, and seminars every year with no "front end." That means, he does not invest money in advertising or direct mail or anything else to get a customer of his own from scratch. Instead, he spends his time finding and forming good working relationships with hosts, who already have customers. To give you a quick idea of the power in this, here are actual net profits from several host/parasite campaigns Ted has engineered, each covering only a 4- to 6-week period of time: $57,000.00, $15,000.00, $30,000.00, and—gulp!—$210,000.00.

I will summarize Ted's key thoughts about host/parasite marketing:

1. Businesses spend fortunes finding and rounding up customers.

2. You can eliminate your out-of-pocket costs, risks, and experimentation by simply paying a host to allow you to be a beneficial parasite, to use the customers that already exist.

3. Host and parasite cooperate to exploit the value in the customers in a way that host couldn't or wouldn't do on his own.

4. Make it easy for the host to say yes. It should involve little or no work for the host, so you need to have sales letters and materials, Web site material, in-store signage, and whatever else is needed for the sale done, tested, proven, and furnished to the host, so he does not have to invest time or money creating anything. You need to guarantee customer satisfaction, so the host does not endanger his reputation.

5. Make it an irresistible financial win for the host. And I would emphasize here, do *not* be a cheapskate about this. Consider what it costs you to get a customer on your own!

6. When you have a success, nurture the relationship so you can repeat the same promotion or do other promotions with that same host, and use that host as a testimonial when you approach other possible hosts.

---

### Resource!

If you happen to be an information marketer like Ted Thomas and me, with books, courses, seminars, coaching programs, etc., to market, you should know that Ted is the king of joint venture marketing in our industry. He has written a Free Report: The Joint Venture Advantage, which you can request by fax at 321-449-9938. There is also additional information about joint ventures and host/parasite marketing for all types of businesses in the free 12-Week Ultimate Marketing Plan Course at *www.UltimateMarketingPlan.com.*

---

# Maximizing Total Customer Value

When you ask a group of businesspeople to list their assets, they quickly write down such items as equipment, furniture, leasehold improvements, and inventory. Many never get around to listing their customers. This lapse is often reflective of trouble in their businesses.

In every *successful* business, the customer *is*, is *perceived* as, and is *treated* as the most important asset. To really get to that point and "own" that belief, you have to figure out what your customer is worth to you, and what your customer can or should be worth to you.

For a period of four or five years, I bought well over half my clothes from one store; suits, sports jackets, slacks. I'd say my average annual purchases at this store have been $4,000.00. In five years, I was worth $20,000.00 in gross. I was also responsible for bringing two business associates and one client to that store, none as good a customer as I've been, but each worth at least half that much. So let's call them $6,000.00 a year, total. Obviously, just as I brought them in, they each have the potential of bringing in additional customers. For the sake of example, let's use a reduced amount; let's say they'd bring in additional customers worth $1,500.00 a year, total.

All together, $11,500.00 a year . . . $57,500.00 every five years.

This store lost me as a customer over this incident: A Sansabelt suit I bought there, I think for $400.00, was, in my opinion, defective. The fabric itself sort of rippled or pimpled after only a few wearings and dry cleanings. I brought it back and asked them to show it to their Sansabelt factory rep the next time he was in to see them, and to "work something out for me." I didn't demand anything. I left it open for them to respond to me with some kind of offer.

After a month, I dropped in. They didn't bring up the suit. I had to ask. The answer was: "Sorry—there's nothing we can do."

So for $400.00 or less, they kissed off more than $50,000.00 in the next five years. They just never thought through the math.

Bill Glazer, the publisher of my *No B.S. Marketing Letter*, owns two thriving menswear stores in Baltimore (Gage Menswear), consults with menswear retailers, and provides complete marketing assistance to thousands of all kinds of retailers nationwide. Many learn from and replicate the elaborate and sophisticated customer retention system that Bill designed for his stores. It involves direct mail, the assignment of an individual sales rep to each customer in an ongoing relationship, and fast, generous complaint resolution. It is not coincidental that he averages a multiple of the average stores' dollars per square foot in sales, has very high, measured customer loyalty, and has withstood both the disintegration of a downtown shopping area around one of his stores and the TV ad–driven assault on his market by a giant warehouse-style menswear chain.

Here's why businesses lose customers:

*One percent die*
Not much that we can do about that—if they insist on dying on us, that's sort of unpreventable and irreversible.

*Three percent move away*
Well, people do move. If they move quite a distance outside our market area, there's not much we can do about that, either.

*Five percent follow a friend or relative's advice and switch to that friend's preferred merchant*
You might be tempted to say there's nothing much to be done about that either, but I'd disagree. How come we lost our customer to his buddy's merchant instead of that other merchant losing his customer to us?

*Nine percent switch due to price or a better product*
Some of this 9 percent can't be prevented, but I'll argue that some could. Why don't we have the best product? Or—if we do—why didn't our customer know that?

*Fourteen percent switch due to product or service dissatisfaction*
True—you just can't please everybody. So some of this is unavoidable, too. But it's my experience as a consumer that a lot of businesses lose me for this reason and are aware of it, but don't even make an attempt to prevent the loss, just like the clothing store I mentioned. Incredibly, they give up without a fight.

But add all that up and you've accounted for only 32 percent of the losses. Why, then, do the majority of customers leave? Can you guess? Sixty-eight percent switch because of what they perceive and describe as indifference from the merchant or someone in the merchant's organization.

In other words, they felt unappreciated, unimportant, taken for granted. Remember, that's not my theory—that's what actual customers have said.

> ## ULTIMATE MARKETING SECRET WEAPON #14
> ## Make the Customer Feel Important, Appreciated, and Respected

On an impulse, a business associate of mine once deviated from our mutual habit of buying and driving Lincolns and bought a BMW—a very, very expensive automobile. The car was a lemon: air conditioning that repeatedly failed, door locks that didn't work, and a bad starter, among other problems. But far more annoying than those things was the way the dealership treated him. Quite frankly, I've never seen anything as outrageous as this dealer's complete, callous, and utter disregard for its responsibilities to this customer. I could tell you story after story, and they all add up to one thing: a car dealer who is wholly ignorant of the concept of Total Customer Value.

Not only will my associate never buy a car there again; he's made certain that I wouldn't, he's talked at least three people seriously interested in BMWs out of going there, and he's still griping to anybody and everybody who will listen.

## How to Do It Right

The story I'm about to tell you comes from an experience I had more than ten years ago. I was struck by it then, I wrote about it in my *No B.S. Marketing Letter*, and I included it in the prior edition of this book. I still have no better example of how to do it right, in such a simple, mundane business—and if this proprietor can do it this well, you can too. So, here's the story. . . .

In Montreal, next to the Lord Berri Hotel, there is a parking lot (or at least there was some years back). If you stay at the hotel, you park there for a daily fee, or by the hour if you're doing business in the area. It is an unpaved lot with a little ramshackle hut where the attendants sit, wait, and listen to a cheap AM radio hung on a nail. In the winter, they shiver and thaw their hands over a portable space heater; in the rain, they huddle and try to dry out between customers; in the summer, they sweat, relieved only by a small electric fan.

There's nothing distinctive about this parking lot. And it's not the kind of place where you expect anything above minimal service.

This particular evening, an associate and I had finished conducting a seminar in the hotel and had gone to the parking lot to retrieve our rental car to go in search of a good restaurant.

On the stool, leaning against the hut, was a guy wearing a T-shirt. The Parking Lot Guy. Nothing distinctive about him; no different than the guys in T-shirts you might run into in any parking lot in any city in the United States or Canada. But this Parking Lot Guy is an exciting reminder that you dare not judge all books by their covers. This Parking Lot Guy should probably be running General Motors.

"Where do you gentlemen want to go with your car tonight?" he asked. We explained that we were heading for an Italian restaurant we'd found advertised in a magazine.

"No," he said, "you don't want to go there. There are much better Italian restaurants much closer, even within walking distance."

A fifteen-minute conversation then took place. He politely quizzed us about our preferences. He got out a telephone directory and called several restaurants to determine how late they were serving, what their specials were, even what wine they had in stock. Finally, we settled on a restaurant a few blocks away. He drew us a map and carefully gave us directions.

If this hasn't shocked you, you haven't done much traveling, and you haven't parked in many parking lots. This guy—for $7.00 a day to park our car—was taking better care of us than the staffs and concierges of most hotels we've stayed in, at $100.00, $150.00, or even $200.00 a day.

He was polite, concerned, friendly, and knowledgeable. We told him so. This is what he told us:

> That's my business; that's what I sell: I'm in the service business. If I can help a person or make friends with a person when he brings his car here the first time, then the next time he has to park his car downtown, he'll remember me and my place. He may even tell somebody else to park his or her car here. If he comes back a number of times, then I'm building a stable business. Then he's not worth a few dollars to me; he may be worth a hundred dollars to me in a year. In my lifetime, he could pay to send one of my kids to college for a year. If I have enough of that kind of customer, then I have a truly valuable business. You can't do that just by parking cars. There are hundreds of car lots. They've all got parking spaces. We have to give service.

I know that's what he said, because as soon as I got seated in the restaurant, I wrote down his words as I remembered them, while it was all fresh in my mind.

It is, I think, a sad commentary on the state of business and customer service in general in our society that the very best example I can put on a pedestal for you to emulate is The Guy in the Parking Lot. But in my book, he wins hands-down.

## The Attitude of Gratitude

I think the kind of customer service that makes customers feel important, appreciated, and respected begins not as policies and procedures but, instead, as an attitude of gratitude.

I was in a doctor's office one day when he asked his receptionist, "What's our body count today?" And that's not uncommon. I've heard customers called bodies, numbers, marks, even chumps. I've seen owners and managers rage on and on about how miserable their customers are—in front of their staffs! These attitudes have to translate into actions, as all attitudes do.

Although it may sound simplistic, getting maximum total value from your customers begins with valuing them totally!

## Make Everyone on Your Team an Ambassador of Customer-Service Diplomacy

To excel in customer service, every member of your team has to understand, accept, and live it as a priority.

Is the customer always right? Surely you've heard that adage: the customer is always right. But you don't have to be in business very long before you know how totally false that is. Although they are thankfully a minority, some customers are grossly unreasonable, some virtually impossible to satisfy. Taking a "the customer is always right" approach to customer service dooms your efforts before they begin. Neither you nor the members of your team will be able to live up to that ideal. I'm not even sure that you should if you could. From time to time, there'll be a customer you will be better off without. I have occasionally "terminated" customers and clients in my businesses, I think for good cause, and I always found that the vacuum quickly filled with better business.

A better, more accurate approach comes from customer-service training expert, Frank Cooper, who says, "The customer signs your paycheck." With that in mind, we can design a Customer-Service Diplomacy Program that makes sense but doesn't force us to aspire to the unattainable.

Diplomacy is all about being gracious, sort of "old-world gracious." If you've ever been to a very formal party at a very wealthy person's home, an old country club, or an embassy, you know what I mean.

Walt Disney insisted that his customers be thought of, always referred to, and treated as "guests," drawing the analogy that if you treat the customer as you would an honored guest in your home, you'll rarely err.

I'd suggest incorporating these key ideas into your own clearly defined, written, taught, and managed Customer-Service Diplomacy Program:

## 1. Greet the Customer as a Welcome, Honored, Important Guest

This means that the customer can never be an interruption. Those who answer your telephones must be professionally educated in good business telephone manners and must use them.

If you've ever walked up to a cash register in a department store and stood waiting while two salesclerks finished their conversation, you've experienced the opposite of this idea—and I'll bet you resented it.

## 2. Be Able to Answer Customers' Questions Knowledgeably

One of the reasons for the early success and growth of The Home Depot chain of hardware, housewares, and do-it-yourself-product warehouse stores was the surprising helpfulness and knowledge of its employees. Its idea was to give the kind of customer service found in old, sole-proprietor hardware stores, but in a modern superstore environment with discount prices.

If you have staff members who are not knowledgeable experts about your products and services, then they must have a good means of immediately getting an answer for any customer at any time that the place of business is open.

Some years back, while "shopping" some residential communities for a client, masquerading as a customer, I asked one salesman a question like this: "If I give you a deposit today on Property A and then want to change my mind and switch it to Property B before 30 days are up, can I do that?"

The salesman honestly didn't know. He probably should have. But he didn't. And at 4:45 P.M. there was no one he could go to or call to get the answer. So he stalled. Had I been a real customer, this would have been the equivalent of stopping a sale dead in its tracks. (By the way, the correct answer was yes.)

### 3. Prevent Policies from Driving Away Customers

I have given up counting—I no longer know (or care) how many times I've been told, "That's our policy." In most cases, my response is, "I've got a policy, too. My policy is never to spend another nickel with your business after I've been told about your policy."

Of course, you have to have policies. I run businesses; I know that. But you'd better remember this one: as a prison warden, you can make up all the policies you want to because you've got a captive audience—they can't leave. Your customer, however, has "the final option." He can put his money back in his pocket and walk away, never to return. Nothing incenses customers more than being quoted "policy."

The very best policy is to create ways to say yes to customer wants and needs. I've been in restaurants where NO SUBSTITUTIONS is imprinted on the menu in big, bold type; where, if asked, the waitress snaps, "no separate checks." Their policy is "Our way or the highway." An awful lot of basically good customers choose the highway.

### 4. Have a Process for Handling Complaints in Place

This is not the time to play it catch-as-catch-can. An angry, irate, unsatisfied customer on the loose in the marketplace can and often will cause you considerable damage. At the very least, each one will spread the word to a dozen or more present or potential customers. They will take dollars right out of your bank account. At worst, they may also cause you some grief with the Better Business Bureau, the Attorney General, or other bureaucracies. Occasionally, a customer driven over the edge strolls in with a shotgun and does some permanent damage.

You need to have a sensible, step-by-step process decided on and in place for diplomatically handling and attempting to resolve complaints.

---

**ULTIMATE MARKETING SIN #4**
**Letting a Customer Leave Angry Without First Exhausting**
**Every Means at Your Disposal to Resolve the Dispute**

---

The foundation of maximizing total customer value has to be creative excellence in keeping and satisfying customers!

## Regard Customer Retention as a Profit Center

A common failing of businesses small and large is focusing all their resources on getting more new customers but investing little or nothing in retaining customers. I try to get business owners to view retention as a marketing function and as a profit center. As a consumer, I'm dismayed at the number of businesses I've patronized once or twice that never contact me. While they are ignoring me, their competitors pursue me with all the ardor associated with seducing someone new. Here are examples of a few of the many companies and businesses that have never once proactively contacted me after or between transactions:

- The dealer I bought my last new luxury car from, three years ago
- A catering company I spent thousands of dollars with five times
- A hotel I've held seminars at, filling as many as 500 rooms
- The insurance agent insuring my homes and cars
- A book printer I spent over $30,000.00 with in one year
- A cruise line I vacationed with
- A local restaurant I took groups to, with tabs in excess of $3,000.00

Every one of these businesses has lost my patronage and been replaced. It's been some time since they've heard from me. Yet I've not heard from any of them, wondering where I've gone.

Here are two functions that must be part of any Ultimate Marketing Plan:

First, a dedicated customer retention and appreciation program, including frequent contact and communication—a newsletter, greeting cards, useful information, little gifts. I do this personally and have done so for thirty years, with terrific results. Almost all of the marketing advisors to different industries that I coach provide their clients with monthly newsletters to send to their customers—including Dr. Ben Alta-donna, who works with chiropractors; Rory Fatt, who works with restaurant owners; Ron Ipach, who works with auto repair shop owners; Tracy Tolleson, who works with mortgage brokers . . . the list goes on and on.

Second, go after "lost customers." Set up some kind of system to track every customer's activity. Whenever one goes missing for an inordinate length of time, send a letter and a great offer, coupon, or free gift, or pick up the phone and call to find out why that person is no longer purchasing from your business. Big companies with monthly services, like long-distance providers, invest heavily in "save the customer" departments. A marketing consultant who works with that industry, George Walther, wrote about one such example, in which it cost the company about $700.00 to get a new customer. But half of all new customers were dropouts before the seventh month. Company analysts figured that cutting those cancellation losses by just 1/10 of 1 percent would add more than a million dollars to the bottom line. By creating a team of "save the customer soldiers" who talked to anyone calling to cancel service and pursued those who did, the company "saved" $8 million of revenue the first year.

### Resource!

Gold/VIP Member Mitch Carson at Impact Products expertly designs and runs turn-key "customer appreciation gift programs" for a variety of businesses and offers a variety of items ideal for such programs for cafeteria purchase. He removes the excuses for not doing this—too busy, not enough time, can't think of what to do, etc.—by doing it for you! Get information at *www.impactproducts.net*. You can also see examples of different customer newsletters in one of the installments of the free 12-Week Ultimate Marketing Plan Course delivered by e-mail at *www.UltimateMarketingPlan.com*.

In this case, this company should be cheerfully willing to spend up to $699.99 on customer retention efforts each year, per customer. Why? Because they know it costs $700.00 to replace one.

If you know what it costs you to get a new customer (and you should know!), then you should make an intelligent decision about proactively investing in keeping and nurturing your relationship with the ones you have.

## The Four Ways to Increase Total Customer Value

There are only four ways to increase Total Customer Value:

### 1. Increase Average Order or Purchase Size

Restaurants do this by effectively merchandising desserts and take-home treats and other products. Industrial marketers do it by expanding product line use and "upping" the customer to bigger sizes. Mail-order companies do it with "today's telephone specials" offered to the caller after the intended order has been taken.

### 2. Increase Frequency of Repeat Purchase

Using rewards, discounts, frequent buyer clubs, volume rebates, and frequent contact, you can capture a larger share of each customer's expenditures.

Murray Raphel, direct marketing expert and developer of the retail mall in Atlantic City called Gordon's Alley, says, "In Gordon's Alley, we have put together a Gordon's Gold Card program. The criteria is simple: did a customer spend $1,000.00 a year or more with us? If they did, terrific. They are entitled to a Gold Card. Now, what does the Gold Card entitle them to? Lots of nice things, including:

1. A free lunch every month from our Alley Deli.
2. Advance announcements of sales.
3. Special vacation packages—a tie-in with our on-site travel agency.

4. Unadvertised specials. Every once in a while, we'll look over our stock and see we don't have enough for a full-blown sale/reduction, but enough for a select group of customers. That's you, Mr./Mrs. Gold Card.
5. Free gift wrapping.
6. Birthday presents—a special gift from our in-store gourmet shop, and with it a $10.00 gift certificate, which brings them into our store."

Now, I want you to notice two things about Murray's brilliant program: first, it has built-in frequent contact with customers. Two, its every feature works to bring the customer back to the store. Why don't more stores and businesses do this? Why don't groups of noncompeting businesses get together and do this? I dunno.

## 3. Offer Existent Customers a Greater Variety of Goods and Services

These people are predisposed to buy from you. In my *No B.S. Business Success* book, I talk at some length about what I call "the mini-conglomerate approach." Given that getting and keeping the customer is the most difficult and expensive business function there is, it just makes sense to work hard at doing more business with each customer. So, the carpet cleaning company that also offers air duct cleaning, sells premium quality vacuum cleaners and air purifiers, and maybe even owns or is in a strategic alliance with a pool cleaning business, lawn care business, and pest control business, leverages each customer to maximum value.

> **ULTIMATE MARKETING SECRET WEAPON #15**
> **Developing New Products and Services for Existent Customers Instead of Getting New Customers for Existent Products and Services**

## 4. Get Existent Customers to Bring You Their Friends, Relatives, Neighbors, Business Associates, Employees, and Others as New Customers

We'll explore this in detail in Step 10. Suffice it to say for now that referrals can be the lifeblood of a business.

One of the people I work with who does a phenomenal job at *all four ways* to maximize customer value is Platinum Inner Circle Member Ron LeGrand. Ron's $20-million-a-year publishing, seminar, and coaching business caters to real estate investors and entrepreneurs. New "students" are acquired from free seminars, a TV infomercial, radio commercials, direct mail, and Ron's bestselling book, *How to Be a Quick Turn Real Estate Millionaire.* First, to increase the average order or purchase size, Ron's company offers multiday, in-depth training events priced from $3,000.00 to $10,000.00, and they are remarkably effective at moving a customer immediately from a $20.00 to $50.00 book or book and CD purchase to a $5,000.00 second purchase. Second, to increase frequency of repeat purchase, Ron offers a series of seven different "boot camps": for example, one has to do with luxury homes, another with "ugly houses," another with foreclosures. Third, to offer his customers a greater variety of goods and services, Ron encourages his most successful investor-students to record their own "how to" audio and video courses, develop seminars, and offer coaching, marketed through Ron's company. This unusual—and I think, brilliant—attitude about cooperation versus competition gives Ron a virtually unlimited flow of new products of interest to his customers with no work on his part. Fourth, Ron has several programs that encourage students to actively refer other students. If you'd like to see more of what Ron does, go to *www.RonLeGrand.com.*

# Fueling Word-of-Mouth Advertising

Let's begin by recognizing that there is no better new customer than a referral from a happy customer. I don't care what business you're in—this is true. The referred customer has less skepticism and is less price-resistant, more receptive, and more easily sold and satisfied.

Most businesses take referrals for granted. Whatever number of referrals they get, they gratefully accept, but they have no proactive plan for stimulating the maximum number of referrals.

## How Many Referrals Can You Get?

Joe Girard, the author of *How to Sell Anything to Anybody* (and someone repeatedly recognized by the *Guinness Book of World Records*), has a "Rule of 52." It is based on his discovery that the average number of attendees at both weddings and funerals is fifty-two. In marketing to consumers, his contention is that each customer has the potential of referring fifty-two other customers. Even if we cut his number in half, ask yourself: Is your business averaging twenty-six referrals per customer? Probably not—most average anywhere from less than one to three. There is room for improvement.

In business-to-business marketing, the numbers are different. I did some admittedly clumsy but, I think, instructive research: I had executives and business owners in a dozen different industries go through their trade association directories and count the number of people whom they knew (and who knew them) on a first-name basis. The average was thirty-seven. Thus, each business customer has the ability to refer thirty-seven others to a vendor.

## The Way to Get Referrals Is with the "Ear" Formula

Listen, my friends, and I'll tell you how to fuel your word-of-mouth advertising to new, unprecedented levels! All it takes is three simple letters.

### *E* Stands for *Earn*

We have to *earn* our referrals. Walt Disney put it this way: "Do what you do so well that people can't resist telling others about you."

---

**ULTIMATE MARKETING SECRET WEAPON #16**
**Excellence**

---

If there is one "secret" to maximum referrals, it is that satisfied customers do not refer abundantly. Enthused, inspired, awed customers refer in great abundance. If you are just good enough, that's not good enough. If customers get only what they expect and deserve, that's not enough.

Let me tell you about a dentist who multiplied his practice by ten in just one year without even a $1.00 increase in his advertising budget. He caters to children and, after a seminar on creative thinking, he built up a list of 300 things to change in his practice. For example:

1. He redesigned his office to provide maximum comfort to the "short people" who came there. He lowered the reception staff into a pit behind the counter, so they were at eye level with the patients.

2. He hung giant photographs of each dentist and dental assistant along with descriptions of each person's hobbies and interests, so new patients could pick their dentists and dental assistants based on having something in common with them.

3. He gave away free bicycles! Every patient got a "home care follow-through Report Card" for his or her parents to fill out. If the Report Card came back to the dentist with all A's, the youngster got a bicycle. (Imagine—as little Johnny rides around the neighborhood on his new bike and people ask him who got it for him, he answers, "My dentist.")

4. He called each new patient at home the evening after treatment, just to see how the patient was feeling. He called each parent the day after the child's treatment.

5. Each new patient left the office the first time with an autographed 8" × 10" glossy of his dentist and dental assistant!

Guess what? At backyard barbecues, PTA meetings, office lunches— the number one topic of conversation was little Johnny's weird dentist! The dentist's practice multiplied itself by ten purely through word-of-mouth advertising (pardon the pun).

## <u>A</u> Stands for *Ask*

I am amazed at the wimpiness of most businesspeople, salespeople, and professionals when it comes to the simple act of asking for referrals. I believe there is a Biblical instruction about this.

Here are the three best ways to ask for referrals:

### 1. Display and Convey Your Expectations

In doctors' offices, we encourage the use of some kind of "display board" listing the names of the patients who have referred that month. This list says to everyone who sees it: "Our patients refer—we expect you to refer also." It works. And it can be copied by an endless variety of retail businesses.

### 2. Conduct Referral Promotions

Give your customers cards, coupons, or certificates good for gifts or discounts that they can endorse, like a check, and give to their friends and colleagues. Then give away prizes to those who generate the most referrals within a certain period.

A clothing store that used this technique got more than 100 new customers in ninety days in exchange for the expense of one getaway weekend, six new suits as second prizes, and the cost of printing up the certificates.

### 3. Conduct Referral Events

An insurance agent I know throws himself a birthday party each year and invites all his clients and all the friends they care to bring to the bash. It's usually held in a huge tent, with live entertainment, a buffet, drinks, wandering magicians, belly dancers, and all sorts of other goings-on. Hundreds of clients bring hundreds of other people each year—and the birthday boy gets to meet and make friends with hundreds of prospects.

## <u>R</u> Stands for *Recognize* and *Reward*

A favorite story: A guy rows his little boat out to the middle of the lake for a relaxing day of fishing. Up over the side of the boat comes a huge green snake, with a half-swallowed frog sticking out of its mouth. Feeling for the frog, the guy whacks the snake with the oar; the snake spits out the frog; the frog's life is saved—and that makes the guy feel good. But the guy also knows he has just deprived the snake of a meal—and that makes him feel bad. Having no food with him, he gives the snake a swig out of his bottle of bourbon, and the snake swims away happy.

Two minutes later the snake swims back with two frogs in its mouth.

When we recognize and reward a certain behavior, we inspire more of the same. It's true in parenting, in managing employees, and in "managing" customers. When you get a referral from a customer or client, the smartest thing you can do is to make a big, big deal out of it. Call with thanks or send a personal thank-you note or gift.

Not long ago, I got a nice referral from a client. I immediately called the Omaha Steaks company and had them Federal Express a box of steaks to the guy. He called and told me that I was the first person in thirty years to actually thank him for a referral. He's since sent me a small fortune in referral business.

> ## ULTIMATE MARKETING SECRET WEAPON #17
> ### A "Champion"

Earlier in this book I told you about the best car salesman I know, Bill Glazner. He has never yet asked me for a referral, but he is so darned good at what he does that I have sent him several dozen customers. And he has thanked me for every one of them.

In me, he has created a "champion"—a person who champions his cause, who tells everybody about him. A handful of cultivated, appreciated champions can make you rich.

# Creating Short-Term Sales Surges

Each business hits its own times of need when a sales surge is important. It's always preferable to sell your way out of a financial problem than to borrow or to sell off equity. Often that can be done.

Here are the best ways I know to create a short-term sales surge.

## Big Discount, Believable Reason Why

Excess inventory, out-of-date inventory, service time during the off-season . . . such merchandise can often be sold at big discounts, but it's important to remember the current high level of skepticism and cynicism of your public. Many outstanding discount offers fail miserably because the intended buyers "smell a rat."

When you run a fire sale, they'd better be able to see the charred timbers!

When you offer an exceptional savings opportunity, there'd better be a good reason. Here are a few "good reasons":

- We're offering this value only to our best customers, as a reward for their support.
- We're extending this offer only to new, first-time customers.
- Frankly, this is our slowest month and to avoid laying off our great employees we'd rather offer you an exceptional value. (There's an upholstery shop in my city that runs this promotion every July with great success.)
- We've been given a special incentive from the factory, and we're passing that savings on to you.
- We're eager to show you our new (whatever) and thought that offering this exceptional value would be a good enticement.

One of the best "excuses" for a big sale is shown in Exhibit #12, in Bill Glazer's "Flood Ad." I'll reveal two secrets about this ad. One, the severity of the leak was a bit exaggerated. Poetic license. Second, half of the ad cost was subsidized by the insurance agent Bill mentions by name in the ad. But what's important here is that he recognized and capitalized on a golden opportunity.

## Exhibit #12

---

A T I O N                                    The Sun : Friday, April 17, 1998 : Page 5A

# Sprinkler malfunction prompts insurance settlement for Gage.

**Downtown menswear retailer gets greenlight from insurance co. to sell inventory at reduction.**

RETAIL PRESS NEWSWIDE

BALTIMORE—It has been several days since an isolated in-store fire sprinkler malfunctioned, causing gallons of water to cascade onto the first and second floors of the downtown Gage Menswear store. And now, the all-important process of getting back to business is now in full swing.

As part of a major settlement involving policy number M-14170, Selective Insurance, Incorporated, the retailer's insurer announced that Gage would be permitted to sell its entire downtown store's inventory at a 30% discount to the public. Gage General Manager, Armstead Black stated, "The merchandise is still high-quality, top-notch designer apparel—most of which was not directly exposed to water. After being closed for business for a few days, we're anxious

to get back to what we're known for: delivering world-class customer service and impeccable garments at discount prices."

With spirits slightly dampened, store owner, Bill Glazer remarked, "I think people already respect us as a trusted retailer downtown, but even I couldn't imagine being able to sell first-run merchandise for 30% less than our normal low prices."

An insurance company official acknowledged how unfortunate it was for the store's interior to be compromised for a short time with renovation equipment on site. However, he went on to point out, "Since the customer's shopping experience will be a bit less convenient, our recommended 30% store-wide discount is the appropriate action to let Gage return to business, and show its customers how much their patronage is valued.

To comply with Selective Insurance's settlement offer, the downtown Gage Menswear store located at the corner of Baltimore and Liberty Streets, across from the Baltimore Arena will sell its entire inventory of designer suits, sportcoats, dress slacks, dress shirts,

casual wear, and all other merchandise at the sanctioned 30% discount.

At presstime, details remain uncertain as to how long Gage will offer the price reductions. When posed with the question, Bill Glazer looked across the first floor of his sprinkler-washed store and said, "I'm really not sure, but I'm expecting business to be brisk." Glazer added, "We're a reputable, customer-service oriented retailer. That's why we've done well downtown. And in keeping with that honest approach, the right thing to do is pass the insurance settlement on to our customers as a discount."

*Longstanding retailer: With a 52-year history downtown, Gage Menswear stands firm on its decision to pass its insurance settlement on to customers via a 30% store discount.*

## Sweepstakes Winners

Want to get past, inactive customers back into your place of business? Want to get all of your customers in this week? I got this in the mail, and the headline immediately grabbed me:

### FINALLY—YOU ARE A SWEEPSTAKES WINNER

I don't know about you, but I enter all those darned magazine company sweepstakes. I go for the Readers Digest sweepstakes and I buy my weekly lottery tickets—after all, as a character in the movie *Let It Ride* said, "You could be walking around lucky and not know it." In a lot of years, though, I have gone winless. Ed McMahon has not called me. But the headline FINALLY—YOU ARE A SWEEPSTAKES WINNER got me. I read that letter. And if you send a letter to every one of your customers with that headline on it, every one of them will read it.

Now, what should the letter say? Here's an example, courtesy of Gary Halbert:

**John Jones**
1515 Anywhere
Junction, AK 00123

Dear Valued Customer:

I am writing to tell you that your name was entered into a drawing here at my store and you have won a valuable prize.

As you know, my store, ABC Jewelry, specializes in low-cost, top-quality diamond rings and diamond earrings. Well, guess what? The other day we got in a small shipment of fake diamonds that are made with a new process that makes them look so real they almost fooled me!

Anyway, I don't want to sell these fakes because they could cause a lot of trouble for the pawnbrokers around town. So I've decided to give them away to some of my good customers, whose names were selected at random by having my wife, Janet, put all the names in a jar and pull out the winners.

So, you're one of the winners—and all you've got to do is drop in sometime before 5:00 P.M. Friday and you'll have a 1-karat "diamond" that looks so good it'll knock your eyes out!

Sincerely,

John Jones

P.S.: After 5:00 p.m. Friday, I reserve the right to give your prize to someone else. Thank you.

With some variation of this idea, you can get all of your customers to flood your store within a short period of time. Then, if you have new products or special offers ready and waiting, the cash register will ring happily.

## The Red-Tag Sale

"It's inventory clearance time and we're closing all day Friday to go through the store and place new red tags on as many items as possible, each with the lowest price ever offered on it. Only a certain number of each red-tag item will be available, on a first come, first-satisfied basis. The red-tag sale starts at 10:00 a.m. Saturday. Red tags will disappear all day long. The later in the day, the fewer the red tags."

That's the basic pitch for a red-tag sale. These tend to work well once or twice a year for retail businesses.

## Coupons, Double Coupons, and Checks

Lots of people buy the newspaper on certain days just to get all the grocery store and manufacturers' coupons inside. They carefully go through all this coupon-driven advertising and inserts, scissors in hand, with buying on their minds. You can capitalize on this with an ad or insert distributed on this day that is made up of coupons and looks like all the other coupon advertising.

If I had a shoe store, for example, my Sunday newspaper insert might be a page of coupons: one for boys' shoes, one for girls' shoes, one for men's, and so on.

There's usually at least one supermarket in each area that advertises a "Double Coupon Day," when all manufacturers' coupons are accepted and doubled; a fifty-cents-off coupon becomes $1.00 off.

If you accept manufacturers' coupons, this is a promotion worth considering. If not, there may be another way you can use the same idea. You might, for example, send a letter to your customer list in advance of your coupon-type newspaper ad advising them of its impending appearance and giving them a card or certificate that doubles the value of the coupons.

I saw a fast-food chain put up signs outside all of its stores while Burger King, its competitor, was running a big coupon promotion:

*WE ACCEPT*

*BURGER KING COUPONS*

*AND*

*GIVE DOUBLE VALUE!*

If mailing to customers for a special sale, consider enclosing a "real" check, made out to your own store, with the customer's name on it where the signature belongs. The check is redeemable at your store but otherwise useless. There's something psychologically challenging about throwing out a check.

## The Premium Makes the Difference

Find a good source for one or more very desirable, appealing premiums and you can build a surge around the "free gift" you offer.

"Gift with purchase" was invented by cosmetic industry pioneer Estée Lauder. It remains the staple of that business. Visit department-store cosmetic counters and you will find that just about every brand has gift-with-purchase offers. In the retail menswear industry, where the norm is discounts, Bill Glazer has consistently produced superior results with gift-with-purchase, as well as gift-just-for-coming-in.

Television sets and jewelry are very effective premiums, particularly around Christmas. Getaway weekend packages work well for car dealers. The most interesting premium I've ever seen: a free Mustang convertible with purchase of a Rolls-Royce.

One outstanding source of low-cost premium merchandise is the closeout merchandise industry. This industry has its own trade shows, newspaper, and catalog companies.

Many of my clients in sales fields, such as financial advisors, insurance salespeople, real estate agents, and business-to-business sales professionals also use gift-with-appointment, to get to the desired decision-makers. Some years ago, I encouraged a sales rep for a software system for dentists to send out a prospecting letter with a toothbrush enclosed to gain attention. The letter offered a 6-foot-high giant toothbrush as a gift for just twenty minutes of a dentist's time to demo the software. He got nine appointments for every ten letters sent—and they called him!

---
### Resource!
---

An expert at sourcing and using a wide variety of premiums is worth his weight in gold! My clients rely on Mitch Carson, at *www.impact products.net.*

---

Two of the most successful premium-driven promotions I've seen in years were put together by my Gold/VIP Member Mitch Carson.

The first item is a beautiful set of imported cultured pearls. The real thing, for a shockingly low cost. Mitch has designed terrific Mother's Day and Valentine's Day promotions using these as free gifts for restaurants, clothing stores, even chiropractors.

Another application of an item like these pearls is gift-for-appointment. Joel Bauer, author of the book *How to Persuade People Who Don't Want to Be Persuaded*, sent a DVD showing the pearls along with his sales letter, both inside a bank bag. He offered the pearls as the "bribe" for an appointment. That produced $1.3 million of trade show bookings for his company!

You can see the pearls and sample promotions at *www.impactproducts. net/pearls.*

The second promotion is very innovative. An association of financial planners, called Piece Of Pie, wanted something unique to use in a monthly gift program for its senior clients. Mitch sourced a variety of authentic foreign bank notes at an affordable cost. He put together a beautifully appointed three-ring leather binder that, with the first of the collectible bank notes, is given to the client as a premium for attending a seminar or coming to a private appointment, and becoming a client. Then, each month, the client receives the next, different currency item encased in hard plastic, ready to be inserted in the notebook, along with a Certificate of Authenticity from the American Numismatic Association. Every month, the client looks forward to the next arrival, curious about what distant land it will be from. The seniors are proudly showing their currency collections to their friends, sparking conversations that are producing referrals. And the entire program—the client lists, fulfillment, and shipping—is all handled for the financial planners by Mitch's company, so it is certain to get done without distracting the financial planner or his staff from their work. You can see this entire program at *www.worldcurrencyprogram.com.*

## The "My Accountant Thinks I'm Crazy" Sale

Sometimes humor works in marketing. I've used this myself, in sale promotions for my mail-order company, and I've seen both retailers and service providers use it effectively.

A tongue-in-cheek ad or letter talks about your annoyance at your nagging, domineering, penny-pinching Scrooge-ish accountant, how he bullies you, pushes you around, and watches you like a hawk . . . but now that he's out of town on vacation for the week, you're going to have some fun, with the wildest, most generous offers in the history of your business.

## Sports-Related Promotions

America loves its sports activities, and sports are always on the minds of a lot of people, so tie-in promotions get favorable attention. For several years in a row, I ran a "triple play" promotion for my mail-order company, offering a "buy one, get two free" deal to my best customers. This is the same as a 67 percent discount, but three for one sounds a lot bigger. And I tied the whole thing to baseball, either early in spring or at World Series time, with free baseball cards, baseball terminology, and clip art, and so on. *IT'S TRIPLE PLAY TIME* pulled as much as a 70 percent response from my customers!

## Trade-Ins

Trade-in promotions are, of course, standard in the automobile business and common with sewing machines, vacuum cleaners, and automobile batteries—but there are lots of other businesses that could use this technique, including office equipment; television, stereo, and electronics; and clothing, with the trade-ins going to the Salvation Army. A spa selling memberships could accept old exercise equipment.

## Easy Payment Terms

If you cover your costs, why not finance your profits? Let's say you want to feature and sell a $300.00 item that costs you $100.00. You might offer your customers this deal: $100.00 down, then four monthly payments of $50.00 each, no interest, no carrying charges. Just have them place their VISA card, MasterCard, or American Express Card numbers with you and sign a simple statement authorizing you to charge their credit cards each month automatically.

You can apply the same structure to hitting a certain size of purchase: buy $500.00 or more and we'll finance two-thirds of the sale.

# New Marketing Technologies

Some of the newest technologies offer tremendous opportunities for creative marketers. Here are my favorites.

## The Nonthreatening First Contact

A prospective customer or client sees your ad or receives your mailing and is interested but, for one reason or another, still reluctant to call you directly and ask questions. Why not offer this person an option—a nonthreatening first contact. There are voice-mail services and systems that will play recorded messages of any length and, if desired, take messages or, at the caller's option, which is indicated by pushing a number, transfer the caller to your main number.

Using one of these recorded messages, you can advertise that main number and give people the option of hearing additional details. Using recorded messages, you can make this information accessible 24 hours a day, 7 days a week. Using recorded messages, you can run smaller ads, thus saving money.

Let's take the auto repair shop owner who wants to advertise in the newspaper, but can't afford to run ads big enough to tell his story. So he runs this relatively small ad:

*BEFORE YOU GO ANYWHERE FOR AUTO REPAIRS:*
*FREE RECORDED MESSAGE REVEALS*
*FOUR SECRETS TO GETTING YOUR MONEY'S WORTH*
*CALL: 555-0000*

My client Craig Proctor, for more than ten years one of the top ten RE/MAX real estate agents in the entire world, pioneered the use of such free recorded messages in his profession, and today, thousands of agents use his ads and recorded message scripts. Successful users of my kind of marketing in many other industries—chiropractic, dental, carpet cleaning, home remodeling, travel, business opportunities—use free recorded messages as well. The leading vendor providing toll-free numbers, recorded messages, transcription of leads and related services is Automated Marketing Services (AMS); you can get the company's information at *www.findmeleads.com*.

──────────── **Resource!** ────────────

Automated Marketing Services has provided a lengthy report, "How to Attract and Capture More Leads, Prospects or Customers and Totally Automate Your Marketing," free to everybody enrolling in the free 12-Week Ultimate Marketing Plan Course delivered by e-mail, at *www.UltimateMarketingPlan.com*.

## Tele-Seminars

For a number of years, people like me—speakers, business coaches, consultants—have routinely used tele-seminars or tele-conferences not just as a means of delivering information, but also as a highly effective and efficient means of selling products and services. But I've had considerable success encouraging others from diverse businesses to use them, too. Chiropractors, dentists, financial advisors, and many others periodically invite all their unconverted leads to an "informative" tele-seminar, where they present information, interview individuals providing testimonials, and answer questions.

Selling via tele-seminars has three great virtues. First, it's very efficient: you can talk to fifty people at a time instead of one at a time. Two, there's safety and anonymity for the listeners, so it is a much less threatening next step for them than is talking or meeting one-on-one. Third, it can even be automated; a tele-seminar conducted live can be recorded and replayed as if "live" again and again.

## Smart Ways to Use the Internet

The Internet is a horribly overhyped area of opportunity. But I can suggest several tested, proven, practical, and almost universally valuable uses:

First, create a Web site for your business, not so much as a means of acquiring customers via cyberspace, but as a customer service, education, and information center. For example, I helped one manufacturer cut down incoming calls from customers with questions about assembly, use, and troubleshooting by nearly 40 percent (saving more than $100,000.00 annually in staff expense) by putting answers to all the commonly asked questions along with diagrams, etc., on a Web site that is accessible free, twenty-four hours a day. You can even make a portion of your site "access restricted," for customers, clients, subscribers, or "members" only, adding mystique to your marketing, and adding perceived value for your clientele. A restaurant could do this with "secret recipes" and special VIP offers; a clothing retailer, with etiquette and fashion tips and special offers; and so on. Of course, you'll also want a promotional area on your site designed for new customers, and you'll then want to add your Web site address to your advertising and marketing materials.

Second, begin collecting and organizing the e-mail addresses of your customers and collecting the e-mail addresses of visitors to your site.

With this list, you can do virtually free, pushbutton marketing anytime you like, as often as you like. You can send out an e-mail newsletter to your customers, or other information, such as tip sheets.

Let's say you have a rather ordinary business; heating and cooling repair, for example. Here are a few of the things you might transmit by e-mail to your customer list:

1. Prepare for winter/prepare for summer info
2. Insulation and energy efficiency tips
3. Long-term weather forecasts gleaned from Farmers' Almanac
4. Special offers for seasonal checkups, maintenance plans
5. New-product information

Exhibit #13 is a simple example from Bill Glazer: a weekly e-mail sent to thousands of customers of his menswear stores. He keeps it brief and simple, in question-and-answer format.

Third, in seeking publicity from the media, being able to fax, e-mail, or mail *very* brief, provocative news releases that refer the recipients to your Web site for more information is very useful.

Everybody in the media is online. And, bluntly, they're lazy, so if they can research a story without leaving their chairs, believe me, that's the way they're going to do it. If you go the route of writing articles for publication in your industry journals, you can even post a whole collection of them on your site, and invite any publication to download and use whatever it likes.

**Exhibit #13**

---

## Kendra Jo Murphy

| | |
|---|---|
| **From:** | Gage Menswear |
| **Sent:** | Thursday, October 14, 2004 12:32 AM |
| **To:** | kendra Murphy |
| **Subject:** | kendra, French cuff dress shirts.... |

Hello Again kendra,

Your weekly fashion Q&A and money saving opportunity from Gage Menswear is here...

Q: What does the Menswear Maven think about French cuff dress shirts?                    M.S., Severna Park

A: Don't miss the chance to add some intrigue around your wrists. French cuffs and cuff links they demand are an instant class transfusion. Unfortunately, most men wear them only at very formal or black-tie events where everyone else will be sporting them as well. Instead, break our from the herd and wear them when nobody else would dare. This doesn't mean at the PTA meeting: but the office will be just fine.

Join Our Repeat Rewards Program and Save Every Time You Shop! Sign-Up For FREE-No Strings Attached
For directions and store hours click here:
http://www.gagemenswear.com/

Notice: You are receiving this e-mail because you requested notification of money saving opportunities at Gage Menswear or because you subscribed (or someone subscribed with your address) when you were in the store. We have the following information on file:
Name: kendra Murphy
Email:
Click the link below to stop receiving these tips and updates:

---

Here is a summation of my recent advice to most business owners about the Internet: Do NOT be seduced, do NOT buy into the hype and expect miracles or invest inordinate amounts of time or money. Do NOT let the Internet take away from your commitment to more reliable, predictable, results-measurable advertising and marketing media. But DO get involved. At whatever pace is comfortable for you, begin learning about the Internet, getting your business on the Net, and experimenting with practical applications like those I just described. Proceed calmly, deliberately, strategically.

With that basic advice dispensed, I've also provided you with a new bonus chapter following this one, from one of the most respected and celebrated experts in Internet marketing, Corey Rudl of the Internet Marketing Center. Corey has made millions via multiple online businesses, beginning humbly and simply with a site selling information about how to intelligently buy a car. At present, he attracts over 1.6 million visitors to his Web sites every month, and all of his Web sites and Internet businesses combined produce over $40 million a year in revenue. I might mention that Corey rarely puts in any time in his office. In fact, it is in Vancouver, British Columbia, and he spends most of his time on the beach in California or traveling to race cars.

Thousands of entrepreneurs have launched online businesses and thousands more promote their offline businesses online following Corey's strategies. Step 13, provided by Corey, could prove extremely valuable and maybe even liberating!

Also, I've secured some advice for you about online advertising from my Gold/VIP Member Perry Marshall, the smartest person that I or any of my clients have ever found when it comes to Google AdWords.

Every day, half a billion—that's billion, with a "b"!—searches are done on the Internet, each one a specific request by someone trying to answer a question or solve a problem. The number one search engine used is Google. And you can advertise on Google. Here's how it works:

Let's say you sell cordless phones. Go to *www.google.com*, click on "advertising programs," and open an AdWords account. You write an ad, then pick a list of keywords that trigger the ad to appear—such as "cordless phone." You set a bid price, which is the maximum price you'll pay for a "click" on your ad. Ten minutes later, your ad starts to appear, driving traffic to your Web site.

―――――――――――――― **Resource!** ――――――――――――――

Perry Marshall offers a free tutorial on Google AdWords, which teaches how to use this medium, how to reduce costs, how to do market tests, and common beginners' mistakes to avoid. You can sign up for this free tutorial at *www.perrymarshall.com/google*.

―――――――――――――――――――――――――――――――――――――――――――

Underneath this simple explanation, there's a very sophisticated game of keywords and bidding strategies, and the rules seem to change daily. There's also terrific opportunity to quickly and cheaply test different ads and offers. That's where Perry Marshall comes in. He's a consummate player of this game, optimizing response for his clients and teaching others how to do it for themselves.

One of the most interesting aspects of Google advertising is how small changes in these tiny, brief ads make big differences. Here are actual split-test examples provided by Perry Marshall:

**Ad #1—0.5% response**

Active Summer Camp: Kids develop learning skills in a fun filled learning environment. *www.SuperCamp.com*

**Ad #2—2.0% response (400% improvement)**

Active Summer Camp: kids develop learning, listening and communication skills at active camp. *www.SuperCamp.com*

Another, for business-to-business:

**Ad #1—0.1%**

> Popular Ethernet Terms. 3 Page Guide—Free PDF Download.
> Complex Words—Simple Definitions. *www.bb-elec.com*

**Ad #2—3.6%**

> Popular Ethernet Terms. Complex Words—Simple Definitions. 3
> Page Guide—Free PDF Download. *www.bb-elec.com*

In this case, in Ad #1, the "thing," the offer, was first, the benefit second. In Ad #2, the benefit was first, offer second.

The third, and last, example:

**Ad #1—0.8%**

> Simple Self Defense For Ordinary People. Easy Personal Protection
> Training. *www.tftgroup.com*

**Ad #2—1.3%**

> Simple Self Defense For Ordinary People. Fast Personal Protection
> Training. *www.tftgroup.com*

The only difference: easy versus fast.

One of the truths about marketing, and certainly about direct marketing, is that the best answer to any and every question is: test! Perry's methods coupled with Google AdWords offers a fast and cheap testing ground for a lot of marketing messages.

## More Will Listen Than Will Read

As a consultant, I've developed "audio brochures"—promotional audio-cassettes or audio CDs—for franchisors and business-opportunity marketers, service businesses, ad agencies, investment counselors, newsletter publishers, planned-community developers, politicians, and dozens of other marketers. In the multilevel marketing industry, more than 2 million copies of the audio brochures I've created have been distributed. A well-done audio brochure offers a number of important advantages, notably these:

## 1. Many More People Will Listen Than Will Read

Right now, about one-third of all adult Americans are functionally illiterate, and that number includes both blue-collar and white-collar workers; both dropouts and college grads; both men and women. I once worked on a TV infomercial starring *Lethal Weapon* actor Danny Glover promoting an adult literacy course and have had the opportunity to talk with many illiterate adults as well as some of the experts in this field. I can tell you that this is a problem no marketer can afford to ignore. There's also a convenience factor at work here: We are a very busy society and many people will not invest their time in reading a solicitation. They will, however, listen.

## 2. High Perceived Value

Recipients value an audiotape or CD—it is not "junk mail" or just another brochure. People are unlikely to discard it without listening.

## 3. Control of Your Presentation

It's difficult to skim an audio presentation. Most people listen to it from beginning to end. You control the order in which they get your information. You can deliver it with voice inflection, enthusiasm, and even music and sound effects.

## 4. Ability to Deliver a More Complete Presentation

An audio brochure can deliver about 250 words a minute; that's 2,500 words in ten minutes, and 7,500 words in thirty minutes. Prospects will listen to ten-, twenty-, and thirty-minute audio messages—it's much tougher to get them to read 2,500 to 7,500 words!

## 5. Repetition

Our own experience and that of our clients indicates that many prospects listen to an audio brochure several times and then respond positively. You might say that they are getting themselves sold, at their own pace.

A good audio brochure can be professionally recorded and produced for under $1,000.00 in nonrecurring costs, then duplicated for sixty cents to $1.00 each.

# Video Brochures and Infomercials

The most powerful medium on earth is television. Want proof? Monica Lewinsky's two-hour TV interview by Barbara Walters not only shot Monica's tell-all book to the top of the bestseller lists, but in a rather odd demonstration of this media's influence, it made the brand and shade of lipstick Monica was wearing the number-one selling lipstick in America overnight.

HBO had a comedy series called *Dream On*, in which lead character Martin Tupper thought in soundbites and images from all the TV sitcoms and movies he watched while growing up plunked in front of the set for hours each day. He responded to just about every event by seeing and hearing a clip from one of the old shows. It was a clever premise and a very funny program, but it is also a powerful reminder of just how much we are influenced by television.

Because we are conditioned to watch talk shows for information and entertainment, a unique advertising medium—the thirty-minute-long infomercial—has turned into a multibillion-dollar industry relying on the talk show format to sell everything from self-improvement courses to car polish.

I've been involved with the production of nearly a hundred of these infomercials, many featuring Hollywood and sports celebrities, and can attest to their incredible power. Shows I've worked on, such as those for Acne-Statin and Proactiv, which are both acne treatments, have literally created huge brands and businesses that have reach far beyond the TV screen.

There are opportunities for smaller businesses, too. For local or regional marketers, infomercials can be aired on local broadcast stations, local cable operations, and regional superstations such as WGN. A local chiropractor has a show he produced for under $10,000.00 that airs in a local market at $500.00 to $700.00 per half hour—with an average payoff of two to three times his media cost in new patients. I produced an infomercial for an Arizona gubernatorial candidate who aired it repeatedly on local broadcast stations throughout the state to get his message out—as well as to raise funds directly via an 800 number advertised on the show. While I can't claim it got him elected—he lost the primary—it did garner a significantly larger vote than he would otherwise have gotten, and it did raise funds. It's now my conviction that given a less controversial, less damaged candidate, such a show would have paid for its media time in direct contributions, dollar for dollar, thus giving the candidate free advertising. I believe you'll see infomercials growing in use for political campaigning. My friend and colleague, Lee Milteer, has played the host in a series of infomercials produced and aired by a group of Virginia Beach cosmetic surgeons, and the shows have created so much business that they can be aired only in short spurts, then rested. Car dealers, travel companies, charities, and an ever-increasing variety of marketers are finding ways to profit from infomercials.

The infomercial duplicated as a video brochure is also proving immensely successful as a recruiting tool for multilevel or network marketing companies, and as a sales tool for car manufacturers, computer companies, health-care practitioners, seminar marketers, and a seemingly endless variety of other businesses.

## Resource!

If you are serious about producing a highly effective video brochure or infomercial, I invite you to contact me personally for assistance or referral to appropriate experts and vendors. Turn-key budgets that include my involvement in writing and producing the infomercial or video run from $100,000.00 to $300,000.00, depending on specifics, and whether or not a celebrity host is utilized. To contact me, fax 602-269-3113.

One such video brochure that I produced for a client is an infomercial-format presentation for a company that builds, sells, and installs backyard sheds, The Shed Shop, in northern California. The video itself features testimonial interviews with different shed owners, at their homes, showing off the sheds and the different uses they make of them—a pottery workshop, a home gym with exercise equipment, an artist's studio, and, of course, storage. Sending the video out with the other literature mailed to prospects responding to the company's advertising has produced not just one, but three positive results: improved response, measured by the number of prospects who come into show rooms; two, improved conversions, measured by the number of prospects converted to buyers; and three, support for higher prices.

## Telemarketing by Robot

One of the most exciting, productive, and low-cost media to have come along in years is voice broadcast. For pennies per delivered call, you can have what sounds to the recipient like a personal phone message, delivered to hundreds, thousands, or tens of thousands of customers with the push of a button.

These work best when they fool the recipient, so you have the service bureau deliver the message only to answering machines and voice mail; it hangs up if a human picks up the phone. Here's how it works. You come home at the end of the day and find four messages on your machine, light blinking. Here they are:

#1: Hi, this is Bob. I just got a satellite dish installed. Want to come over and watch every NFL game this Sunday? Call me.

#2: Hi, this is Charley. Can I borrow $100.00 until payday? It'd really help out. I lost $300.00 in a poker game and Carol doesn't know. I'll pay you back. I swear.

#3: Hi, this is Hal, your dry cleaner. Sorry I missed you. I wanted to let you know about a special sale just for our VIP customers, starting tomorrow. You won't see it advertised anywhere. You can bring in drapes, bedspreads, furniture covers, throw rugs, anything like that and get one item dry-cleaned free for every two you bring in. This is only for you, and only tomorrow through Monday. Oh, and I've got a coupon for a free Subway sandwich for you, too.

#4: Hi, it's me. I'll be home late. Go ahead and eat without me.

Here's what's very important: You can't tell that call #3 is any different than #1, #2, or #4. You think Hal the Dry Cleaner called you personally.

A legal note: There are laws about this, as there are for all kinds of telemarketing, robotic or not. Generally speaking, you can make these kinds of calls to your established customers, and under certain circumstances, you can make them to prospects who've requested information from you, but you can't make them en masse, "cold" to people with whom you have no relationship.

One of the best users of these kinds of calls for a retail business is Bill Glazer. He's used calls in his voice, and then, as his customers caught on, began using celebrity-impersonated voices to deliver his calls as "Elvis," "Bill Clinton," and others.

_____ **Resource!** _____

I've arranged for you to hear actual samples of a number of these voice broadcast calls at *www.instantvoicepromotions.com*. This is a great opportunity to learn more about a terrific marketing medium you may not have used—one that could be a key to huge sales increases!

## Broadcast Fax

For the past handful of years, one of the most productive and profitable marketing tools the majority of my clients have been using is broadcast fax. Unfortunately, recent changes in laws, as well as instances of civil litigation, have all but ruled this out as a medium for contacting people you lack relationship with or don't have permission from. However, most of my clients are still able to use it a lot with their own customers, clients, members, and with prospects they obtain permission from. You should check with your lawyer, with the Federal Trade Commission at *www.ftc.gov,* or with other resources about your particular applications.

Here are some examples of very productive uses:

- **Restaurants:** weekly specials and events calendar; seasonal promotions for holiday parties, catering, etc.; coupons sent to regular customers.
- **All Businesses:** an offer with an impending deadline. We've had great success with what I call "countdown faxing," which delivers a different fax each day, day after day, three, four, or five days from a deadline. Headlines saying "Only 5 Days Left," "Only 4 Days Left," "Only 72 Hours Left," "Only 48 Hours Left" are prominently emblazoned across the top.
- **Reminder Notices:** for people who've registered to attend a tele-seminar, seminar, or meeting of some kind. You can deliver a reminder notice precisely timed—the day before or the hour before the event.
- **Timely Information:** fast, even same-day response to current news events. For mortgage brokers and Realtors: an interest rate change. For a sporting goods store: a promotion tied to who won the Super Bowl or World Series, sent minutes after the game.

_____  **Resource!**  _____

Companies that can provide voice broadcast and fax broadcast services can be found in the expanded Resource Directory at *www.dankennedy.com.* The vendor most used by my clients is Automated Marketing Solutions (AMS), at *www.findmeleads.com.*

# How to Make the Internet Work for You

*By Corey Rudl*
*Internet Marketing Center*

How would you like to wake up in the morning, grab a cup of coffee, and turn on your computer to discover that you've just had thousands of dollars *automatically* deposited in your bank account? Or lie on a beach knowing that, while you're on vacation, your business is running itself—*automatically* making sales and depositing profits into your bank account?

---

*Note:* Shortly after completing this chapter but before publication of this book, my friend Corey Rudl died in an auto racing accident. He died very young but while doing what he passionately loved. The information in this chapter is just as valid, and the work at the Internet Marketing Center that Corey founded continues under the expert direction of Derek Gehl.

It can happen to you, just as it's happening, right now, to thousands of small and home-based business owners all over North America—people who never imagined they'd be making six-figure incomes! Ordinary people now enjoying incredible prosperity . . . all thanks to the Internet.

## Ordinary and Unusual Businesses Can Profit from the Internet

Absolutely every business can benefit from going online.

It doesn't matter what you sell—whether it's jewelry, real estate, or even swimming pools—by simply putting up a basic Web site (with nothing more than a bit of sales copy and a few relevant pictures) and then using a handful of tested and proven Internet marketing strategies, you are *guaranteed* to make more money!

Let me give you some examples. . . .

Let's pretend that you own a hair salon. Some people may go online to search for a hair salon, but a whole lot more people will probably look in their Yellow Pages, or get a recommendation from a friend.

So why should your salon be online, if you're already listed in the phone book?

Here's why. If you're a smart entrepreneur, every time someone comes to your salon to have their hair cut or colored, you're going to get their e-mail address from them while they are paying you. Then you're going to make note of the date and kind of service you performed for them.

This is extremely powerful information!

Why? Because three weeks from now, when you realize that business is slow, you can simply sit down and write all of your customers an e-mail like this . . .

Dear (insert customer name here):

Thank you for your visit on July 10th, 2005, for the cut and perm.

I just wanted to write and thank you for your business. I also wanted to let you know that for the week of September 17th, 2005, we're offering a special 20% discount on haircuts to all of our valued customers. However, you must book your appointment within the next 48 hours for this offer to apply.

We look forward to seeing you again soon!

Sincerely,

YOUR NAME HERE, Owner

Elite Cuts Hair Studio

This kind of simple e-mail can start your phones ringing and fill your salon quickly.

Will this technique generate more business? Definitely! How much time did it take you? Almost none! Did it cost you anything? No!

Let me give you another example. . . .

Okay, you cut hair for a while and decided it wasn't your thing. So now you own a grocery store. Great! How can being online benefit you? Once again, you can use the Internet to keep in touch with your customers and improve your customer service!

You simply get the e-mail address of every person, letting them know that you'll be sending them online coupons every week. By doing this, you are going to remind thousands of people, "Come back to our grocery store, because we're going to give you thirty cents off yogurt, a dollar off milk . . . ," etc.

Are they going to come back? You bet! Why would they go back to the grocery store down the street that doesn't communicate with them, when you're there, not only keeping in touch with them, but offering them an incentive to come back?!!!

All you need to do is remind them that you're there. And it costs you nothing!

*That's* the beauty of the Internet. It has literally done the impossible—it's given people the power to contact hundreds—if not *hundreds of thousands*—of potential customers literally in seconds, with almost zero cost.

Every business—I don't care who you are or what you do—should be online. If you're not online, you're losing money.

Let's say you want to have a wine and cheese party . . . or you're having your year-end blow-out sale . . . or you want to remind everyone that during the Christmas season they should book their appointments early to avoid being disappointed. You just e-mail your customers in advance to notify or remind them.

Perhaps your salon is starting up a new massage service. With this technique, you could be fully booked the day after you open, simply by announcing it via e-mail.

Is this technique going to make you a millionaire? No, it isn't. Is it going to make you more money? Absolutely! So think about that. Use the Internet creatively. Use it to create the kind of loyalty and rapport that turns a first-time customer into a lifetime customer!

## Even Fifty-nine-Year-Old Grandmothers Now Have Web Sites

Back when I was first starting out, if you wanted to start an online business, it was a very different process than it is today.

If you wanted a Web site, and you were on a tight budget, you had to know HTML and be prepared to do all the dirty work yourself—like figuring out how to make all of your software, ordering systems, and databases work together (ugh!).

Fortunately, these days, getting a Web site and preparing it to accept credit card payments from your customers is much easier, and I still can't believe how cheap it's become!

There are now tools and software that will do it all for you, step by step, often in less than a few hours, and often for a low monthly fee (usually less than the cost of dinner and a movie).

And the best thing is that if you're a newcomer to the world of online business, you have the opportunity to learn from those who have gone before you. You get to benefit from all of our successes and failures, all the trial and error we had to go through during the early days of Internet marketing.

Let me give you an idea of what I mean. . . .

I didn't even know what the Internet *was* when I first got started online. I had to learn everything from scratch. I had to learn HTML programming. I had to figure out the basics of Web site design, mostly through trial and error. And I had to figure exactly *how* to market a product online.

Back then, there wasn't a whole lot of useful information about Internet marketing—there were so few people who were trying to do it. There were no resources for me to consult, no books to tell me what to do. I just had to wing it.

I took the marketing concepts I'd learned from people like Dan Kennedy, Jay Abraham, Gary Halbert, and Ted Nicholas—people who charge up to $15,000.00 for some of their three-day seminars—and applied their techniques to the Internet. I quickly learned that although some offline marketing techniques translated beautifully to the Internet, some were dismal failures. And what really surprised me was that it was virtually impossible to predict which would work and which would fail.

I worked eighteen- to twenty-hour days for *months on end* testing different strategies. I ended up doing so many tests in those early years that I could hardly see straight!

Luckily, *you* don't have to put in this kind of effort. These days, to get started online, you don't need to be a marketing genius or a computer whiz at all. There are resources that are cheap and easily available that will help you take your business online—every step of the way.

Let me ask you this. . . . Can you send and check e-mail on your computer at home? Have you ever typed into *www.something.com* and surfed the Web?

Well, then, congratulations! You have all the technical skills you need to take your business online.

I am dead serious. I know successful online entrepreneurs—people who are making hundreds of thousands of dollars a year, or more—who knew nothing about computers when they first decided to try launching an Internet business.

Let me introduce you to a couple of them. . . .

## "He Was Afraid to Touch a Computer. . . . Now He's Making $1,000,000.00 a Year Online!"

Preston Reuther has faced incredible personal odds to build and grow not just one profitable online business . . . but three of them!

A few years ago, Preston was having a really tough time of it. He was suffering from a serious illness that prevented him from holding down a full-time job outside his home. While in the hospital being treated for his illness, he started making wire jewelry as a hobby. Stuck at home without any way to make money, Preston decided to turn his hobby into an online business.

There was only one problem. . . . Preston didn't know the first thing about computers.

*"At the time, I could not turn the computer on. And when I say I couldn't turn it on, I mean that literally . . . I was afraid to touch the buttons!"* he remembers.

However, that soon changed. Now, just a few years later, Preston and his wife are running Wire-Sculpture.com, a business that generates over $1 million a year!

For Preston, the change came when he bought my course and started following my simple step-by-step lessons on how to get started online.

*"I was just days away from giving up,"* Preston confesses. *"Then I sold over $3,500.00 in goods and services in three days! I now use about 75% of Corey's techniques and my sales are up to $90,000.00 EACH MONTH—very consistently."*

## "He Was a Poor Teenager Living in the Inner City. . . . Now He Makes $500,000.00 a Year—And He's Still in His Early Twenties!"

Jermaine Griggs was living in the inner city and working from a corner desk in his grandmother's living room when he began dabbling online. Building on his piano-playing prowess, he decided to experiment with a Web site called HearAndPlay.com. It teaches clients how to play the piano by ear—through the Internet!

Needless to say, this is not the kind of product one would typically associate with an online business—and yet Jermaine has managed to turn a $70.00 investment into a highly profitable business.

"I started this site in November 2000 and I made just $60.00 that first month," Jermaine says. "It wasn't until March of 2002 that I started making over $5,000.00 a month. That soon doubled and then quadrupled."

Last year, Jermaine reached a whopping $500,000.00 in annual sales, and his business just keeps on growing. And he's still in his early twenties!

"The site has allowed me to become independent from my parents at an early age, while everyone else I know either still lives at home or depends on their parents," he says. "I have been able to live alone, furnish my home, upgrade my music studio, and attend college without worrying about finances."

Preston and Jermaine are proof that you don't need to be a computer programmer or a Web designer or an M.B.A. You don't really need any technical know-how at all! Anyone can start an online business. And everybody can do it successfully.

# How to Take Your Business Online for Less than $25.00 a Month

One of the best things about marketing through the Internet is that it's cheap. You can have a Web site available for the entire WORLD to see for less than a couple hundred bucks!

For example, one of my clients, Jordan McAuley, started his online business when he was going to college full-time. Like most college clients, he barely had two nickels to scrape together. He had to scrimp and save to get the money he needed to launch his Web site—which he did for under $200.00. Now his celebrity contact information site, ContactAnyCelebrity.com, makes $500,000.00 a year!

Another successful client, Dianne Beiremann, spent only $100.00 to launch her "automotive gifts and gadgets" site, PWMEnterprises.com. That's how much it cost her to buy the domain for her site and purchase the initial catalogs from her supplier. She was on a tight budget, so she designed the site herself, even though she had no previous background in Web site design. Within months, her business was making a profit. Now it makes $100,000.00 a year—a thousand times the amount of her investment!

And an online business can be just as cheap to run as it is to start.

Once you have someone's e-mail address and have been given permission to contact them, you can send as much promotional material as necessary to make a sale—FREE! Not only is this a great way for you to turn leads into customers, it's also a fantastic opportunity for you to test copy you can use in your offline campaigns.

Another of my clients, Chad Tackett, is an expert at this. His site, Global-Fitness.com, is a members-only Web site that offers customized meal plans, fitness tracking software, personal consulting, and related information to help his clients achieve their fitness goals. On his site, he offers ten valuable fitness tools that his site visitors can access free of charge. These include a fitness analysis calculator, a nutritional food database that gives nutritional breakdowns for a huge range of foods, and a fat calculator. To use these free tools, his site visitors have to enter their names and e-mail addresseses and opt in or opt out of receiving his free weekly fitness newsletter. More than 80 percent of his visitors choose to opt in—he receives more than 350 subscribers a day!

Thanks to these promotions and other great advertising strategies, Chad's site pulls in more than $1 million a year!

## Paid Advertising on the Internet Costs Pennies!

Did you know that you can BUY traffic from the search engines for literally *pennies*?

It's true! Some search engines allow you to bid for top-ranked listings within their search results. For each person who searches the keywords you've bid on and then clicks through to your Web site, you pay whatever you bid. And keyword bid prices start from only 5 cents a click.

Best of all, when you use "pay-per-click" search engines, you only pay for advertising *that works* because you only pay when someone actually clicks through to your Web site.

Rosalind Gardener of Sage-Hearts.com is yet another incredibly successful entrepreneur I know. She makes over $50,000.00 a *month*, with a whopping 40% to 50% profit margin—and she does this by promoting other people's products!

According to Rosalind, *"Pay-per-click search engine advertising is the ultimate method for getting targeted traffic quickly."*

## Your Internet Business Can Run Automatically— *While You Sleep!*

If you're not familiar with the ins and outs of running an online business, the extent to which you can automate your business will probably astound you.

With an online business, it's now possible to automate most of your sales process. You can also automate many of your advertising tasks *and* much of your communication with leads and customers. This will save you literally dozens of hours each week—time you can spend *growing* your business instead of running it!

Take my client, Bert Ingley, for example. He runs VGSports.com, an online business that sells strategy guides for a number of popular video games. His video guides are electronic "eBooks" that can be delivered to customers *instantaneously* right over the Internet. Bert has automated his entire sales process so he doesn't have to be involved in closing the sale or delivering his product at all. Best of all, delivery doesn't cost him a dime—and his business makes well over *$350,000.00 a year!*

*"Thanks to all the great automatic tools, it takes us only 14 hours a week or so to run our business,"* Bert says. *"The rest of the time is spent writing and researching new products—in other words, playing the heck out of new video games!*

*"I'm now able to work at home and spend quality time with my wife, two boys and baby girl,"* he says. *"Because the business is so fully automated and able to run itself for extended periods of time, I can go on vacation or take time off without the whole business grinding to a halt."*

Automation even helps you increase your sales.

You can send out automatic "follow-up" e-mails to customers who have recently made a purchase that tell them about other products you sell that complement the one they just bought, and give them a discount if they buy right away. By offering them a deal and creating a sense of urgency, you can immediately increase your revenues by 30%! How much extra money would 30% be for YOUR business?

## Reach Millions of New Potential Buyers from Every Corner of the Globe

Maybe the most profitable aspect of taking your business online is being able to get the word out about your products or services to a *much* larger audience. . . .

With an online business, you have the opportunity to advertise your products and services to entirely new markets, all around the world, for absolutely NO extra cost.

Take Larry Dague of ScubaToys.com, for example. He runs a diving gear shop in Dallas, Texas, hundreds of miles away from the nearest ocean—*not* exactly the best place to sell scuba gear. However, thanks to the great Web site he's developed, his business makes *$4 million a year!* According to Larry, a lot of business owners think that a Web page is a great way to bring their stores into people's homes. But for him, it's a great way to bring people into his shop!

*"I'd say over 80% of the people who walk into my store do so because they found it on the Net,"* he says. *"Many times I've had a customer drive in from up to 300 miles away with a printout of our Web pages. They come into the store and point at the printout and say, 'I want two of these, and three of these. . . .'"*

Larry's site averages 150,000 unique visits a month—and many of these site visitors become buying customers.

Here's an example of how impressed people are by his products and services: A man living in Ohio ordered a full set of gear from Larry's online store. His town has a population of less than 2,000 and doesn't offer much in the way of dive shops.

The man liked his gear so much, he bought another full set for his wife a week later. Within two months, eight of their friends and relatives had also bought products from Larry. In the course of a year, Larry sold more than $18,000.00 worth of scuba gear to that one little Ohio town!

Larry says that his Web site has also had a major impact on the amount of local business he gets. *"The larger our Net presence grows, the stronger influence it has on the local area. . . . We have become known as 'the place to buy' in Dallas."*

The Internet also makes it especially easy to find and communicate with niche markets. The best thing is, these niche markets may seem small when confined to a particular geographic location, but they're huge when considered globally. Your business can be much more specialized than it would be otherwise.

Let's say you sell pet supplies. The Net makes it easy for you to target dog owners, cat owners—even rare-bird owners—and tell them about your products. It's much harder (and a *lot* more expensive) to do this offline.

One of my clients, Taylor Knight of YourParrotPlace.com, is a perfect example. She has a Web site that sells pet supplies exclusively to parrot owners. Her online business generates $100,000.00 a year!

Can you imagine running a business like that offline? How many parrot owners do you think there are in your hometown? Probably not enough to keep a $100,000.00-a-year business afloat!

Thanks to the Internet, your business no longer has to be confined to a particular location. You can sell your products to anyone . . . anywhere . . . anytime. When it comes to marketing a product, geographic borders have become a thing of the past.

_____ **Resource!** _____

The Internet Marketing Center's complete Course, *The Insider Secrets To Marketing Your Business On The Internet*, contains over 1,000 pages, including step-by-step, illustrated instructions to build, automate, and create traffic for your Web site and, for advanced marketing, to turn an existent Web site into a "money machine." Go to *www. marketingtips.com/kennedy* for details about the Course. Also, one of the lessons in the 12-Week Ultimate Marketing Plan Course delivered by e-mail has been prepared by Corey, and you can enroll free at *www.UltimateMarketingPlan.com*.

# Avoid Employee Sabotage:
# Getting Employees on the Same Page

Here's a nasty little "secret" that isn't much of a secret. Every business owner knows it, but most prefer to ignore it, like ostriches with their heads buried in sand, or indulge in denial, preferring to believe that these kinds of problems only happen in the other guy's business. But here it is: In 99.9 percent of all businesses, the owner's Ultimate Marketing Plan, the effective advertising, is undermined and sabotaged by the employees!

I want to try to give you some fresh, provocative perspective on this.

First, your employees are MEDIA, just like your Yellow Pages ad, Web site, sales letter, and store signage. They convey marketing messages a myriad of different ways, in their attitude, dress, personal hygiene, body language, smile, adherence to scripts for answering the phone, greeting customers, upselling, enthusiastic support of offers advertised, and on and on. When they are on board and operating in a way that is totally congruent with your marketing, they can have enormous positive impact. But when they are not on the same page—when, behind your back, they are deviating from your prescribed ways of doing things—they can destroy your business. You have to *make them* congruent. You must tolerate nothing less.

Second, a lot of your headaches, frustrations, and disappointments with your employees are your fault, not theirs. Business owners have naive, unrealistic, and unreasonable expectations about their employees and employee behavior. Because the owner thinks about his business all the time, it's hard for him to remember that his employees think about it as little as possible!

My good friend and business colleague Lee Milteer, a business and performance coach to entrepreneurs, provides a comprehensive system for getting owners and managers and their teams working together. She counsels the owners via telecoaching sessions. She provides support to the staff via audio programs and other resources. She has worked with some of the best big companies in America, including FedEx, Disney, and the NASA space program, as well as thousands of small businesses. More than fifty different leading consultants to different industries enroll all their business-owner clients in her Millionaire Mindset Coaching Program, and as of this writing, its participants number more than 15,000. I've asked her to contribute a few comments to this chapter, so the rest of this is from her:

You invest a lot of time and money in advertising and marketing to make the phone ring or make new customers walk in the door. The bad news is, all too often, that money and effort goes right down the drain because you have not taken the time to educate your employees—who interact directly with those customers—on what marketing is being done, why it's being done as it is, and what you expect to occur. You leave the employees unprepared and in the dark, they resent it, and they strike back. Sometimes, with visible rebellion. Sometimes, with secret sabotage.

Further, even if you do lay out exactly the way you want your advertising, marketing, sales, and customer service to link seamlessly together, and you do train your people on what is expected of them, your intentions will never come close to the reality that occurs and that customers experience if you fail to supervise and police.

Think about the last time you walked into a store or other place of business and saw the big sign that says: Our Customers Are The Most Important People On Earth! Yet twenty minutes later you are still vainly searching for someone who works there to help you. Three clerks are clustered together in a conversation with each other. When you do get one to pay attention, the clerk's blatant lack of interest turns you off. You are clearly an interruption, a nuisance.

These problems begin with employees getting "what to do" training but never getting "how to think" training. By that I mean, "right thinking." People have to be told, taught, and motivated to think about their jobs, their customers, their roles, and themselves in a way that will support your intentions and objectives.

The idea of "ownership mentality" is a myth, impossible to sustain. You need to face the fact that employees cannot and will not think like you think, or think like owners think. If they did, they'd be owners. They are going to think like employees. And if you're not careful, they will think like the worst employees think. *It's no skin off my nose if that customer leaves frustrated or angry and goes someplace else—my paycheck's the same at the end of the week. These customers keep interrupting my work. The owner is an idiot. Our prices are way too high.* These kinds of things are heard behind owners' backs constantly.

In many businesses, the employees are actually running the show. Dan Kennedy tells me of business owners who abandon great marketing plans with the explanation: *My employees won't do it. My employees don't like it.*

You have to adopt the "there is a new sheriff in town" mentality—put on your badge, take control of your business, and be a real leader. This involves several different roles. Leadership is the development of marketing, of sales, and of customer service plans and procedures, laying out the vision, the goals, the way things are to be done. Training is teaching, coaching, helping people understand and adopt the practices you want used. Supervision is being a cop—frequently, constantly checking up, to see that things actually are being done as intended. For training to be effective, it needs to be an ongoing process, not a one-time thing nor an occasional, erratic response to things gone awry. Layered on top of that, both managers and staff need "mindset training" to help them handle stress, be better communicators, value teamwork, and take pride in achieving goals.

Most business owners invest the least time and money in their people, who have the direct personal contact and influence with their customers, clients, or patients. Instead, they invest most of their resources in their facilities, equipment, products, and advertising and marketing. But the return on all those other investments actually hinges on the performance of the people!

---

### Resource!

---

For information about Lee's *Small Business Guide to Employee Effectiveness for Owners and Managers*; the *Keys to Performance Excellence and Career Success* employee kit; training programs, seminars, tele-coaching, and private performance improvement coaching for entrepreneurs, go to *www.milteer.com.*

---

# Hiring and Firing the Experts

The typical businessperson will face a whole array of experts eager to help him or her—for a price. These notably include advertising agencies and marketing consultants. I have owned an ad agency, I am a marketing consultant, and I'm going to tell you that you've gotta watch out for us!

My friend and colleague Bill Brooks defines "consultant" as somebody who knows 357 sexual positions but can't get a date for Friday night. It's not an unfair characterization.

## You Are the Expert

My very best word of caution is this: remember that you are the number one expert in your business. Nobody has the feel for it that you do. And you must never let a hired gun talk you into doing something that feels totally wrong to you. Trust your instincts.

Also, I suggest using experts to do a better job of what you could do if you had to. I think you need to know enough about advertising, marketing, and promotion to do your own before you turn it over to other experts. This way, you can tell good from bad and right from wrong.

It frightens me when a client delegates 100 percent of his marketing decisions to me or some other outsider. I prefer working as a collaborator by matching my marketing expertise with his unequalled understanding of his own business.

> ### ULTIMATE MARKETING SIN #5
> ### Abdicating Control

If a consultant gets huffy about explaining his reasoning and rationale for his suggestions and his work—shoot him. (Or, at the very least, fire him.) You have a right to pass judgment on his reasoning.

## How to Hire an Advertising or Marketing Pro

Before you hire an expert, determine that the person's expert status comes from experience, not theory. I am constantly amused by the consulting firms and ad agencies that employ people directly from college—I'd never, ever, hire such a person. There is a night-and-day difference between solving marketing problems in the classroom and in the real world; there is a red-and-green difference between creating an ad in six weeks in the classroom and figuring out how to fix a headline in six minutes under the deadly deadlines of real life. The big-name firms who hire wet-behind-the-ears MBAs do their clients a grave disservice.

I suggest you hire experts with real-world experience: somebody with bruises and battle scars, who started out at the broom-in-hand level and clawed his way up. Determine whether or not he knows how to sell.

Incidentally, I happen to be one of the highest fee, highest paid direct-response copywriters in America (based on copywriters' fees published in the industry directory "Who's Charging What"), and I know most of the top pros. And I know a little secret nearly all of us share. We have some kind of direct, face-to-face, nose-to-nose, toes-to-toes selling experience. Vacuum cleaners, water filters, encyclopedias, pool cleaners, insurance, something. We know how to sell and transfer that to the different marketing media we work in. I advise great caution in letting anyone work with you or for you on your advertising and marketing who lacks such experience.

Let me tell you a little secret about a lot of ad agencies: they hire outside consultants to help them prepare presentations to new clients because, without help, they can't even sell their own services!

Determine whether or not your expert has successful *direct-marketing* experience. That means that, through print or broadcast, he has managed to get people to go to the phone or mailbox and exchange their hard-earned bucks for his products. Any goof can create good institutional (image) advertising. This is no-brainer stuff. Worse, nobody can measure whether it's good or bad. I'd like to hear Goodyear's story of *exactly* how much revenue is produced as a result of the blimp.

Ad agencies love institutional advertising. They hate direct response.

Most ad agencies like to get paid by fees and a percentage of all the money the client spends buying media. Good direct-marketing pros like to get paid based on the sales or results of the campaigns they create. That tells you a lot.

Determine whether or not the marketing professional you're thinking of hiring has some experience with a business, product, or service similar to yours. I turn down clients with businesses I have no feel for and experience with, and I call that integrity. In the rare cases where I deal with a business that is totally foreign to me, I freely disclose that to the client and I appropriately discount my compensation. I call that integrity, too.

## Warning Signs of Experts to Avoid Like the Plague

Not long ago, I was brought in to try to fix an infomercial that had been badly botched by its producers and had proven to be a gold-plated flop. Sitting in the editing facility, I was grumbling and ranting and raving, wondering out loud how anybody could louse up a production so bad.

The editing engineer said, "Let me answer that. The producer told me he thought this project was a loser and his objective was to use the client's money to his own best advantage, to get a few clips that would make his portfolio look good."

Every time I go into an agency with a wall full of awards, I wonder whether they're working for their clients or the award committees. It is worth mentioning that a lot of the advertising that wins awards performs poorly. Agencies that win awards often lose the clients involved in the award-winning campaigns.

Some of the most productive, profitable advertising and marketing in the history of the planet could never qualify for any of the awards. Much of the best marketing gets its results in an ugly way. There may even be a formulaic relationship of awards to profitable results for clients. If there is, it'd be: the fewer awards, the better the clients' results.

Along these same lines, an aversion to long copy and a love of "white space" is a dead-bang giveaway of an inept expert.

I was once having lunch with a client of mine and with a guy who was trying to sell my client on joining a new advertising co-op. The co-op guy spent ten minutes criticizing my client's current ad, telling him it was too cluttered, had much too much copy, and so on. When he finally shut up, my client innocently responded: "Well, maybe you're right. It only pulls an eight-times return on investment. How much better do you think your group will do?

The poor guy almost needed the Heimlich maneuver.

Take a look at the work being done by the pro you're thinking about hiring and see how closely it conforms to the principles presented in my book *The Ultimate Sales Letter*. If your pro's copywriting methods differ greatly from those described in my book—run! That may sound arrogant, maybe even closed-minded, but that's just the way it is.

Now here's the big danger signal: refusal or reluctance to provide a number of satisfied, successful clients you can call and talk to. Certainly there are instances in which confidentiality precludes a consultant from revealing clients. That does exist. But it is the exception, not the norm. Any ad agency or marketing pro worth his salt should be able to provide a number of good references and, when checked out, those references should be thrilled with the work of the consultant. Anything less than this is simply unacceptable. Get and check references.

# How to Get More Information from the Author

**<u>FREE STUFF LINKED TO THIS BOOK!!!!!</u>**

To help you get full value from this book,

there is a collection of

## FREE EXTRA RESOURCES

waiting for you at

*www.UltimateMarketingPlan.com:*

**FREE E-Mail Course** . . . extension of the book – enroll today!

**FREE Tele-Seminar** with the Author

**FREE Ultimate Marketing Plan Tool Kit**

. . . and every other extra resource referred to throughout this book.

# ENTER THE NATIONAL SALES LETTER & MARKETING PLAN CONTEST

Compete for a new FORD MUSTANG and other exciting prizes!

Have your best sales letter/marketing plan evaluated by a panel of expert judges

No purchase required

Contest is connected to two new 2006 books by Dan Kennedy: *The Ultimate Sales Letter* and *The Ultimate Marketing Plan*

All rules, details, and Free Registration at:

*www.NationalSalesLetterContest.com*

# ATTEND FREE!

## —The Ultimate One-Day Marketing & Wealth Creation Training Conference

**$995.00 Per Ticket**
**Public Price**

**This Coupon Valid For TWO FREE TICKETS**
**TO REGISTER: go to *www.UltimateMarketing Plan.com*, find the Conference information and use Code# NBSW**

**THIS ONE TIME ONLY CONFERENCE** features Dan Kennedy, Bill Glazer (on "Outrageous Advertising"), Paul Hartunian (on "Free Publicity"), Ron LeGrand (on "Multiple Income Streams"), Yanik Silver (on "Internet Opportunities"), and other outstanding speakers and experts. This is a limited time offer. If you are purchasing the book after the Conference (late 2006), you will receive an alternate gift.

# Special Free Gift From The Author

Copy this page and FAX to 410-727-0978
Or go to *www.Ultimate-Sales-Letter.com*

**FREE: Test Drive Three Months of Dan Kennedy's
Gold Inner Circle Membership**

*Includes:*

1. Three months of the *No B.S. Marketing Letter*
2. Three months of Exclusive Audio Interviews
3. Three months, Marketing Gold Hotsheet
4. Gold Members' Restricted Access Archives Web site
5. Million Dollar Resource Directory

There is a one-time charge of $5.95 to cover postage for ALL three months of the FREE Gold Membership, and you have no obligation to continue at the lowest Gold Member price of $39.97 per month ($49.97 outside North America). In fact, should you continue with Membership, you may later cancel at any time.

Name _____ Business Name _____

Address _____ __ Business __ Home

City, State, Zip _____

E-Mail _____

FAX _____ Phone _____

- - - - - - - - - - - - - - - - - - - - - - - - - - - - - - - - - - - - - - - - - - - - - - - - - - - -

__ AmericanExpress    __ VISA    __ MasterCard

Card# _____ Exp Date _____

Signature _____ Date _____

Providing this information constitutes your permission for Glazer-Kennedy Inner Circle LLC to contact you regarding related information via above listed means.

# WEB SITES OF SPECIAL INTEREST

*www.dankennedy.com*
Information about Dan Kennedy professional services, newsletters, and audio products. Also, Glazer/Kennedy Inner Circle annual Marketing And Money-making SuperConference and annual Information Marketers' Summit.

*www.renegademillionaire.com*
Information about Dan's Renegade Millionaire System and annual Renegade Millionaire Retreat.

*www.nationalsaleslettercontest.com*
Information about the sales letter/marketing plan contest, featuring a new Ford Mustang as top prize. No purchase required to enter.

*www.nobsbooks.com*
Information about all books in Dan Kennedy's No B.S. series, free sample chapters, bonus gifts for each book, and free e-mail courses.

*www.petetheprinter.com*
Home of DONE4YOU publications and services, including ready to use customer newsletters for any business, featuring Dan Kennedy content. Also, two special Dan Kennedy publications: *No B.S. INFO-Marketing Letter* (only for information marketers) and *Look Over Dan's Shoulder* (for direct response marketers and copywriters).

# Other Books by Dan Kennedy

<u>*Companion to this book:*</u>
*The Ultimate Sales Letter* (Adams Media)

<u>*The No B.S. Series*</u>
*No B.S. Sales Success* (Entrepreneur Press)
*No B.S. Business Success* (Entrepreneur Press)
*No B.S. Time Management For Entrepreneurs* (Entrepreneur Press)
*No B.S. Wealth Attraction For Entrepreneurs* (Entrepreneur Press)
*No B.S. DIRECT Marketing For NON-Direct Marketing Businesses*
(Entrepreneur Press)

*Make Millions With Your Ideas* (Plume)
*The New Psycho-Cybernetics with Dr. Maxwell Maltz* (Pearson)
*Zero Resistance Selling* (Prentice-Hall/Pearson)

*The Ultimate Success Secret* (*www.dankennedyproducts.com*)
*Why Do I Always Have to Sit Next to the Farting Cat* (petetheprinter.com)
Complete Catalog Of Audio Programs: *www.nobsbooks.com*

# Resource Directory

In this Resource Directory, you will first find people mentioned in the book whom you might want to contact, listed in order of first appearance, by page number. You will also find a second section, with contacts and vendors in category groups. A much more extensive, frequently updated Resource Directory is provided to all Glazer-Kennedy Inner Circle Members who receive my *No B.S. Marketing Letter.* You can arrange a free three-month membership with no obligation at *www.UltimateMarketingPlan.com.*

Bill Glazer, President, Glazer-Kennedy Inner Circle, Inc.,  page x
Mitch Carson, CEO, Impact Products,  page x
Craig Dickhout, Think Ink,  page x
Corey Rudl, CEO, Internet Marketing Center,  page x
Kevin Fayle,  page 11
Bob Higgins, Higgins Painting,  page 18
Scott Tucker, Tucker Family Financial,  page 37
Darin Garman, Real Estate Marketing Systems,  page 37
Dr. Barry Lycka,  page 52
Dr. Charles Martin,  page 52
Rory Fatt, Restaurant Marketing Systems,  page 57
Jerry Jones, Jerry Jones Direct,  page 63

Tracy Tolleson, Tolleson Mortgage Publications, Inc.,　page 64

Bill & Steve Harrison, Bradley Communications Corp.,　page 97

Dr. Paul Hartunian,　page 99

Joe Polish, Piranha Marketing,　page 106

Lester Nathan, Results Management & Marketing, Inc.,　page 111

Chauncey Hutter Jr., Real Tax Business Success,　page 112

Ted Thomas, Trevor & Jones Marketing,　page 128

Dr. Ben Altadonna,　page 140

Ron LeGrand, Global Publishing Inc.,　page 143

Craig Proctor,　page 160

Perry Marshall,　page 164

Lee Milteer,　page 169

## Platinum Members

### Dr. Chris Brady

The Brady Group
3940 Timber Lane
Colorado Springs, CO 80908
Phone: 719-495-3168
Fax: 719-466-9119

### Craig Brockie

Defining Presence Marketing Group
2707–83 Garry Street
Winnipeg, Manitoba R3C 4J9
CANADA
Phone: 204-982-0011
Fax: 604-648-9673

### Rory Fatt

Restaurant Marketing Systems
7198 Vantage Way
#104
Delta, BC V4G 1K7
CANADA
Phone: 604-940-6900
Fax: 604-940-6902
Web site: *www.roryfatt.com*

### Jay M. Geier

Scheduling Institute
1875 Old Alabama
Suite #845
Roswell, GA 30076
Phone: 770-518-7575
Fax: 770-518-7577

**Bill Glazer**
Glazer-Kennedy Inner Circle, Inc. & BGS
Marketing
407 West Pennsylvania Avenue
Towson, MD 21204
Phone: 410-825-8600
Fax: 410-825-3301
Web site: *www.bgsmarketing.com*

**Bill & Steve Harrison**
Bradley Communications Corp.
135 E. Plumstead Avenue
Lansdowne, PA 19050
Phone: 610-259-1070
Fax: 610-259-5032

**Reed Hoisington**
Reed Hoisington Pub. Inc.
2413 Morganton Road
Fayetteville, NC 28303
Phone: 910-484-4519
Fax: 910-485-3524

**Chauncey Hutter Jr.**
Real Tax Business Success
504 Old Lynchburg Road
Suite #2
Charlottesville, VA 22903
Phone: 434-220-4705
Fax: 434-220-4706

**Ron Ipach**
Cinron Marketing Group
7908 Cincinnati-Dayton Road
Suite #0
West Chester, OH 45069
Phone: 513-779-3660
Fax: 513-779-4990

**Alan Jacques & D. J. Richoux**
Business Breakthrough Technologies
4058 Wellington Street
Port Coquitlam, BC V3B 3Z7
CANADA
Phone: 604-552-9431
Fax: 604-552-9429

**Jerry Jones**
Jerry Jones Direct
1020 Shipping Street NE
Salem, OR 97303
Phone: 503-371-1390
Fax: 503-371-1299

**Michael Kimble**
Group M Marketing Inc.
9433 Bee Cave Road
Bldg. 2, Suite 110
Austin, TX 78733
Phone: 512-263-2299
Fax: 512-263-9898

**Ron LeGrand**
Global Publishing Inc.
9799 Old St. Augustine Road
Jacksonville, FL 32257
Phone: 888-840-8389 / 904-262-0491
Fax: 888-840-8385 / 904-421-0182
Web site: *www.RonLeGrand.com*

**John Paul Mendocha**
Speed Selling
11800 Della Lane
Grand Terrace, CA 92313
Phone: 909-783-4400
Fax: 909-370-1170

**Internet Marketing Center (Corey Rudl, Derek Gehl)**
#400–1155 W. Pender Street
Vancouver, BC V6E 2P4
CANADA
Phone: 604-730-2833
Fax: 604-638-6015

**Ted Thomas**
Trevor & Jones Marketing
3525 N. Courtney
Suite B
Merritt Island, FL 32953
Phone: 321-449-9940
Fax: 321-449-9938

**Yanik Silver**
Surefire Marketing Inc.
10832 Brewer House Road
N. Bethesda, MD 20852
Phone: 301-770-0423
Fax: 301-770-1096

**Dr. Robert Willis**
The Coaching Program
5908 E. 106th Street
Tulsa, OK 74137
Phone: 918-688-8848
Fax: 918-298-7943

## Resources by Category

### PUBLICITY

**Bill & Steve Harrison**
Bradley Communications Corp.
135 E. Plumstead Avenue
Lansdowne, PA 19050
Phone: 610-259-1070
Fax: 610-259-5032
Web sites: *www.FreePublicity.com* and
*www.NationalPublicitySummit.com*

**Dr. Paul Hartunian**
P.O. Box 43596
Upper Montclair, NJ 07043
Phone: 973-857-4142
Fax: 973-857-4140
Web site: *www.Hartunian.com*

### DIRECT MAIL

**Mitch Carson**
Impact Products
5331 Derry Avenue
Suite J
Agoura Hills, CA 91301
Phone: 888-215-4758
Fax: 818-707-1777
Web site: *www.impactproducts.com*

**Craig Dickhout**
Think Ink
19891 Beach Blvd.
Suite #35
Huntington Beach, CA 92648
Phone: 714-374-7080
Fax: 714-374-7071

## MARKETING TECHNOLOGIES

**Ron Romano**
AMS
230 Watline
Mississauga, ON L4Z 1P4
CANADA
Phone: 800-858-8889, Ext. 124
Fax: 888-629-6622
Web site: *www.findmeleads.com*

## INTERNET MARKETING

**Perry Marshall**
1508 Ridgeland Ave.
Berwyn, IL 60402
Phone: 708-788-4461
Fax: 708-788-4599
Web site: *www.perrymarshall.com/google*

**Yanik Silver**
Surefire Marketing Inc.
10832 Brewer House Road
N. Bethesda, MD 20852
Phone: 301-770-0423
Fax: 301-770-1096

**Internet Marketing Center (Corey Rudl, Derek Gehl)**
#400–1155 W. Pender St.
Vancouver, BC V6E 2P4
CANADA
Phone: 604-730-2833
Fax: 604-638-6015

## EMPLOYEE MOTIVATION, TEAM BUILDING

**Lee Milteer**
Lee Milteer Inc.
3882 Jefferson Boulevard
Virginia Beach, VA 23455
Phone: 757-460-1818
Fax: 757-460-3675
Web site: *www.milteer.com*

# SPECIALIZED MARKETING ADVISORS
## For Accountants and Tax Professionals

**Chauncey Hutter Jr.**
Real Tax Business Success
504 Old Lynchburg Road
Suite #2
Charlottesville, VA 22903
Phone: 434-220-4705
Fax: 434-220-4706

## For Auto Repair

**Ron Ipach**
CinRon Marketing Group
7908 Cincinnati-Dayton Road
Suite O
West Chester, OH 45069
Phone: 513-779-3660
Fax: 513-779-4990

## For Carpet Cleaners and Other Service Businesses

**Joe Polish**
Piranha Marketing
2318 S. McClintock Drive
Suite #1
Tempe, AZ 85252
Phone: 480-858-0008
Fax: 480-858-0004

## For Chiropractors, Cosmetic Surgeons, Dentists, Cosmetic Dentists, and Other Professional Practices

### Dr. Ben Altadonna
Altadonna Communications
322 W. Prospect Avenue
Suite B
Danville, CA 94526
Phone: 800-795-5221
Fax: 925-314-9442

### Dr. Chris Brady
The Brady Group
3940 Timber Lane
Colorado Springs, CO 80908
Phone: 719-495-3168
Fax: 719-466-9119

### Jay M. Geier
Scheduling Institute
1875 Old Alabama
Suite #845
Roswell, GA 30076
Phone: 770-518-7575
Fax: 770-518-7577

### Jerry Jones
Jerry Jones Direct
1020 Shipping Street NE
Salem, OR 97303
Phone: 503-371-1390
Fax: 503-371-1299

### Dr. Barry Lycka
780–10665 Jasper Avenue
Edmonton AB T5J 3S9
CANADA
Phone: 780-425-1212
Fax: 780-425-1217
Web site: *www.cosmeticsx.com*

### Dr. Charles Martin
11201 Huguenot Road
Richmond, VA 23235
Phone: 866-263-5577
Fax: 804-320-1014
Web sites: *www.AffluentPracticeSystems.com*, and *www.MartinSmiles.com*

### Dr. Robert Willis
The Coaching Program
5908 E. 106th Street
Tulsa, OK 74137
Phone: 918-688-8848
Fax: 918-298-7943

## For Direct Marketing for All Businesses

### Dan Kennedy
5818 N. 7th Street, Suite #103
Phoenix, AZ 85014
Phone: 602-997-7707
Fax: 602-269-3113
Web site: *www.dankennedy.com*

### Michael Kimble
Group M Marketing Inc.
9433 Bee Cave Road
Bldg. 2, Suite 110
Austin, TX 78733
Phone: 512-263-2299
Fax: 512-263-9898

### Ted Thomas
Trevor & Jones Marketing
3525 N. Courtney
Suite B
Merritt Island, FL 32953
Phone: 321-449-9940
Fax: 321-449-9938

## For Independent Pharmacies

### Lester Nathan
Results Management and Marketing Inc.
1222 Godfrey Lane
Nickayuna, NY 12309
Phone: 518-346-7021
Fax: 518-346-8325

## For Mortgage Brokers and Lenders

### Reed Hoisington
Reed Hoisington Pub. Inc.
2413 Morganton Rd.
Fayetteville, NC 28303
Phone: 910-484-4519
Fax: 910-485-3524

### Tracy Tolleson
Tolleson Mortgage Publications, Inc.
5818 N. 7th Street, Suite #103
Phoenix, AZ 85014
Phone: 602-265-1922
Fax: 602-269-3113

### Scott Tucker
Tucker Family Financial
2154 W. Roscoe Street
Chicago, IL 60618
Phone: 773-327-3094
Fax: 773-327-2842
Web site: *www.mortgagemarketinggenius.com*

## For Real Estate Agents

### Craig Proctor
Craig Proctor Productions
1111 Stellar Drive, Suite #12
Newmarket ON L3Y 7B8
CANADA
Phone: 905-640-0449
Fax: 905-640-0448
Web site: *www.QuantumLeapSystems.com*

## For Real Estate Investors

### Darin Garman
Real Estate Marketing Systems
3045 Winston Circle
Marion, IA 52302
Phone: 319-350-5378
Fax: 319-373-5535
Web site: *www.commercialinvestments.com*

### Ron LeGrand
Global Publishing Inc.
9799 Old St. Augustine Road
Jacksonville, FL 32257
Phone: 888-840-8389/904-262-0491
Fax: 888-840-8385/904-421-0182
Web site: *www.RonLeGrand.com*

### Alan Jacques & D. J. Richoux
Business Breakthrough Technologies
4058 Wellington Street
Port Coquitlam, BC V3B 3Z7
CANADA
Phone: 604-552-9431
Fax: 604-552-9429

### Ted Thomas
Trevor & Jones Marketing
3525 N. Courtney
Suite B
Merritt Island, FL 32953
Phone: 321-449-9940
Fax: 321-449-9938

## For Restaurants

### Rory Fatt
Restaurant Marketing Systems
7198 Vantage Way
#104
Delta, BC V4G 1K7
CANADA
Phone: 604-940-6900
Fax: 604-940-6902
Web site: *www.roryfatt.com*

## For Retail Businesses

### Kevin Fayle
3621 Wildflower Cr.
Syracuse, NY 13215
Phone: 800-836-3904
Fax: 315-492-0585

### Bill Glazer
Glazer-Kennedy Inner Circle, Inc. & BGS
Marketing
407 West Pennsylvania Avenue
Towson, MD 21204
Phone: 410-825-8600
Fax: 410-825-3301
Web site: *www.bgsmarketing.com*

### Bob Higgins
Higgins Painting
6898 Yvonne Court
Redding, CA 96001
Phone: 530-242-1610
Fax: 530-244-9680

### Lester Nathan
Results Management and Marketing Inc.
1222 Godfrey Lane
Nickayuna, NY 12309
Phone: 518-346-7021
Fax: 518-346-8325

## For Sales Professionals

### John Paul Mendocha
Speed Selling
11800 Della Lane
Grand Terrace, CA 92313
Phone: 909-783-4400
Fax: 909-370-1170

### Lee Milteer—Millionaire Mindset Coaching
Lee Milteer Inc.
3882 Jefferson Blvd.
Virginia Beach, VA 23455
Phone: 757-460-1818
Fax: 757-460-3675
Web site: *www.milteer.com*

# Ultimate Marketing Plan Think-Sheets

Here is a summary of the steps, principles, and ideas presented in the book, to help you develop your own Ultimate Marketing Plan. You may want to go through this exercise annually, every six months, every three months, or even monthly, depending on the size, nature, and maturity of your business. This set has been completed with possible responses for an Italian Restaurant. To obtain a blank set of Think-Sheets for your own marketing plan, sign up for the free e-mail course available at *www.UltimateMarketingPlan.com.*

## MESSAGE

### 1. RESEARCH ON COMPETITION AND SIMILAR BUSINESSES, PRODUCTS, AND SERVICES

Their features, benefits, claims, USPs, etc.:

1. *Intimate, romantic atmosphere*

2. *Award-winning chefs*

3. *Banquet rooms available*

4. *Catering available*

5. *Take-out*

6. *Nightly specials*

7. *Homemade pasta*

8. *Extensive menu*

9. *Fresh seafood daily*

10. *Major credit cards*

11. *Casual atmosphere*

12. _____

13. _____

14. _____

15. _____

16. _____

### 2. FEATURES AND BENEFITS OF YOUR BUSINESS, PRODUCT, OR SERVICE:

| Feature | Benefit |
|---|---|
| 1. *Award-winning chef* | 1. *Chef's Nightly Specials* |
| 2. *Homemade pasta* | 2. *All pasta made daily (fresh)* |
| 3. *Fresh seafood flown in daily* | 3. *Fresh seafood choice every day* |
| 4. *Extensive menu* | 4. *Extensive menu guarantees* |
| 5. *Extensive menu* | 5. *"Something for Everybody"* |
| 6. *Take-out* | 6. *Call ahead and take-out* |
| 7. *Take-out* | 7. *Orders accepted by fax* |
| 8. *Major credit cards accepted* | 8. *All major credit cards welcome* |

9. *Banquet Facilities*     9. *Complete Banquets for 10 to 1,000 people*

10. _____     10. _____

## 3. UNIQUE SELLING PROPOSITION
Describe:

*We offer both a "Gourmet Room" with a formal, candlelight atmosphere and strolling*

*violinists and a "Casual Dining" Enclosed Patio.*

## Write 3 different headlines based on your USP:

1. *Gourmet Italian Dining—Elegant or casual atmosphere.*

2. *Two great Italian restaurants in one.*

3. _____

## 4. IRRESISTIBLE OFFER(S)
Develop one or more irresistible offers compatible with your USP and summarize each offer in 20 words or less:

1. *Lobster and pasta for 2, just $8.95 each, on the patio or in the dining room.*

2. *Free bottle of house wine for each table, Wednesday nights.*

3. _____

## PRESENTATION _____

### 1. THE FIVE STEPS
Explain the need of your customer:

*(1) Dinner     (2) Dining Out*

*(3) Entertainment     (4) Good Food*

## Explain the general "thing" that fulfills that need:

*An evening at a fine restaurant*

## Explain why your product, service, or business is the best "thing":

*An evening at "Giuseppe's" provides fine food, choice of atmosphere*

## Justify your price:

*Less than people expect—many $15.95 complete dinners*

## Give the reasons the customers should act now:

*2-for-1 Special*

## 2. HOW CAN YOU BUILD THE CUSTOMER'S INTEREST IN YOUR PRODUCT, SERVICE, OR BUSINESS?
At least five ideas:

1. *Story about our chef*

2. *Awards won by restaurant and/or chef*

3. *Show: Choice of 2 atmospheres*

4. _____

5. _____

## 3. SET UP YOUR CALL TO ACTION

What do you want the customer to do? (options)

1. *Call for reservations*

2. *Come in*

3. *Call for menu and brochure*

## TARGETS

### 1. DESCRIBE YOUR GEOGRAPHIC TARGET MARKET:

*West side suburbs*

### 2. DESCRIBE YOUR DEMOGRAPHIC TARGET MARKET:

*White collar, upper-middle income*

### 3. DESCRIBE YOUR ASSOCIATION/AFFINITY TARGET MARKET(S):

*Chamber of Commerce*

*Italian-American Club*

*5th Street Merchants Assoc.*

## PROOF

### 1. LIST ALL THE TYPES OF "PICTORIAL PROOF" YOU HAVE:

1. *Photographs of "2 atmospheres"*

2. *Photographs of meals*

3. *Photographs of pasta being made on premises* _____

4. _____

5. _____

## 2. LIST ALL THE "TESTIMONIAL PROOF" YOU HAVE:
Real People:

1. _____

2. _____

3. _____

Celebrities:

1. *The Mayor eats here often* _____

2. *Channel 3's TV Weatherman* _____

3. _____

## 3. LIST THE "REFERENCE PROOF" YOU HAVE:

1. *List of banquet clients* _____

2. _____

3. _____

## 4. LIST THE "DEMONSTRATION PROOF" YOU HAVE:

1. *Taste-test our pasta against "commercial" pasta* _____

2. _____

3. _____

_____

## 5. LIST ANY OTHER PROOF YOU HAVE:

1. *12 years in business at same location*

2. *Awards*

3. _____

## 6. DESCRIBE THE GUARANTEE(S) YOU OFFER:

1. *Complete satisfaction or dinner's on us.*

2. *Guaranteed seating within 15 minutes of your reservation*

3. _____

# IMAGE

## 1. NOTES RE: APPEARANCE OF BUSINESS PREMISES

*2 Atmospheres—Unique*

*Enclosed patio has fountain, flower garden*

## 2. NOTES RE: BUSINESS PREMISES FACILITATING BUYING

*Live lobsters in tank*

*Giant photos of daily specials*

## 3. NOTES RE: COMMUNITY AFFAIRS

_____

_____

## 4. NOTES RE: CELEBRITY SPOKESPERSON(S)

_____

_____

## 5. NOTES RE: BRAND-NAME IDENTITY

*"Giuseppe's Sauce"—in bottles sold at cash register*

## PUBLICITY

## 1. CHARITY/NONPROFIT CONNECTION IDEAS:

*Provide dinner gift certificates for charity auctions*

## 2. PERSONAL SELF-PROMOTION IDEAS:

## 3. POSITIONING AS AN EXPERT:

*Idea—run a weekly newspaper column of chef's recipes*

## 4. CREATIVE PROMOTIONS TO MEDIA:

*Deliver free pasta to all radio hosts during Italian Liberation week*

## 5. TALK SHOWS:

*Write a book—"The Sauce Book"*

## 6. PRESS KIT:

_____

_____

## MALIBU-ISM: STAYING HOT ――――――――――

### 1. PLANNED/BUILT-IN CONSTANT CHANGE

What's New?

* 30 days from now:

_____

* 60 days from now:

_____

* 90 days from now:

_Special Summer "Lite Dining Menu"_____

### 2. SEASONAL PROMOTIONS

To-do List:

_____

_____

### CALENDAR WEEKS:

1. _New Year's Eve Party_____

   . . .

4. _"Australia Week" Shrimp specials_____

5. _Start pushing Valentine's Day_____

6. _Valentine's Day_____

...

8. *Start pushing St. Patrick's Day* _____

9. *Green Pasta—St. Patrick's Day* _____

10. *Promote Easter Dinner Specials* _____

11. *Promote Easter Dinner Specials* _____

12. *Easter Dinners* _____

13. *Italian Liberation Week* _____

14. *Mother's Day* _____

...

19. *Father's Day* _____

...

40. *Columbus Day* _____

41.

42. *Halloween* _____

43.

44. *Thanksgiving* _____

...

47. *Thanksgiving* _____

48. *Holiday Parties* _____

...

52. *Holiday Parties* _____

_____

## "POOR BOY" MARKETING STRATEGIES ───────────

### 1. INBOUND TELEPHONE PROCEDURES:

*Tell about daily Specials*        *Get name, phone, and address*

*Choice of Atmosphere*

### 2. TELEPHONE UPSELL PROCEDURES:

### 3. OUTBOUND TELEMARKETING IDEAS:

*Call past customers*

### 4. YCDBSOYA—Proactive ideas:

*Active in Chamber, Clubs*

*Personally go meet each area business owner*

### 5. CO-OP PROJECTS:

### 6. WINDOW DISPLAYS:

*Tie to seasonal themes*        *Pasta-making machine*

*Lobsters in tank*

## 7. "TEASER" NEWSPAPER ADVERTISING:

*Campaign for "Italian Liberation Week"*

## MAXIMIZING CUSTOMER VALUE ————————————

### 1. HONORED GUEST GREETING PROCEDURES:

*Good Maitre d'*

### 2. PRODUCT KNOWLEDGE—TEAM TRAINING:

*Job rotation*

*Waiters briefing by chef ½ hr. before opening each evening*

### 3. POLICY CONTROL:

*Special orders accommodated if at all possible*

### 4. COMPLAINT-RESOLUTION PROCESS:

*Turn over to Manager*

*"No Charge" meal for any unhappy customer*

### 5. CUSTOMER-RETENTION PLAN:

*Track customer frequency and recency*

*Call "Lost" customers*

## REFERRALS

### 1. *Earn*—Ideas:

*Outstanding waiters (memory courses)*

*Daily "White Glove" inspections*

### 2. *Ask*—Ideas:

*How can we convey our expectations:*

*Monthly events calendar and newsletter with "Thank-you" list of those who referred*

### Referral Promotions:

*"2-for-1 Dinner With a Friend" Cards*

### Referral Events:

*Annual big party, free appetizers, entertainment*

### 3. Recognize and Reward:

*"Thank-you" notes*

*Free appetizer certificate*

## SALES SURGES

### 1. BIG DISCOUNT, REASON WHY—Ideas:

*Special prices for weeknights*

## 2. SWEEPSTAKES WINNERS—Ideas:

*Trip to Italy*

## 3. RED-TAG SALE—Ideas:

## 4. COUPONS—Ideas:

## 5. PREMIUMS—Ideas:

## 6. CRAZY ACCOUNTANT SALE—Ideas:

## 7. SPORTS-RELATED PROMOTIONS—Ideas:

*Monday Night Football, pizza buffet in lounge*

## 8. TRADE-INS—Ideas:

## 9. E-Z PAYMENT TERMS—Ideas:

*Banquets or catered affairs charged to credit card in 3 monthly installments*

## 10. CELEBRITY APPEARANCES—Ideas:

## NEW TECHNOLOGIES

## 1. NONTHREATENING FIRST CONTACT/RECORDED MESSAGE—Ideas:

*Hear menu—daily specials on special phone numbers*

## 2. INTERNET—Ideas:

## 3. AUDIO BROCHURE—Ideas:

## 4. VIDEO BROCHURE—Ideas:

*To area companies to show banquet facilities*

## 5. INFOMERCIAL—Ideas:

_____

_____


## 6. DESKTOP PUBLISHING/MARKETING—Ideas:

*Monthly events calendar*
_____

_____


## 7. ROBOT TELEMARKETING—Ideas:

*Call all homes in nearby suburb with a special offer*
_____

_____


## 8. FOCUS GROUPS—Ideas:

*Survey customers re: new food item ideas*
_____

_____


## 9. EXPERIMENT!—Ideas:

_____

_____

# Index